THE PRACTICE OF MAHAMUDRA

THE PRACTICE OF MAHAMUDRA

THE TEACHINGS OF HIS HOLINESS,
THE DRIKUNG KYABGON, CHETSANG RINPOCHE

Edited by Ani K. Trinlay Chödron

Snow Lion Publications
Ithaca, New York USA

Snow Lion Publications
PO Box 6483
Ithaca, NY 14851 USA
tel. 607 273 8519

Printed in Canada on acid-free, recycled paper

ISBN 1-55939-124-3

Library of Congress Cataloging-in-Publication Data

Chetsang, Rinpoche.
    The practice of Mahamudra : the teachings of His Holiness
Chetsang Rinpoche / translated by Khenpo Konchog Gyaltshen.
        p.   cm.
    ISBN   1-55939-124-3
    1. Mahāmudrā (Tantric rite) 2. Meditation—'Bri-guṅ-pa (Sect)
I. Gyaltsen, Khenpo Rinpochay Könchok, 1946-   .
BQ7699.M34C44   1999
294.3'444—dc21
                                    99-27858
                                        CIP

TABLE OF CONTENTS

ACKNOWLEDGMENTS

His Holiness the Drikung Kyabgon taught the Fivefold Path of Mahamudra in a series of lectures given all across the United States during the spring and summer of 1994. The main body of this book originated in a week-long retreat at the Tibetan Meditation Center in Frederick, Maryland. This was supplemented with material compiled from other teachings given during that tour, all translated by Khenpo Konchog Gyaltshen. We are grateful beyond expression for the kindness of these lamas, who first preserved these teachings in a living tradition, and then generously made them available to us in the West.

This book would not have been possible without the compassionate efforts of:

—Len Marlieb, who tirelessly transcribed a great heap of tapes;

—Rick Finney, Steve Willing, and Tony Romano, who edited, proofread and encouraged many times along the way;

—the members of the Drikung Kagyu centers throughout the country, who assembled the causes and conditions for these profound teachings to be given;

—Lama Konchok Samten, who translated the Long Life Prayer with Dr. Clark; and

—the staff at Snow Lion Publications, who made important improvements to the manuscript and made presentation of this work to the public possible.

By the merit of this work, may all sentient beings attain the perfect, complete, precious Enlightenment!

INTRODUCTION

In the great Dakpo Kagyu lineage, the "blessing lineage,"
there are two systems of Mahamudra practice—the sutra system and the tantra system. In the sutra system, Mahamudra
is described as freedom from elaboration, non-duality, without subject or object. In the tantra system, it is explained as
the inseparable unity of bliss and emptiness, the co-emer-
gent primordial wisdom. Dharma Lord Gampopa empha-
sized practice according to the sutra system based largely on
the *Uttaratantra* teachings from Buddha Maitreya. Because
of this emphasis, Lord Phagmo Drupa taught his disciples
that way, and his lineage comes to us through Lord Jigten
Sumgön, the founder of the Drikung Kagyu. There were many
other great lamas who specialized in this teaching, such as
the Third Karmapa Rangjung Dorje and the Eighth Karmapa
Mingyur Dorje from the Karma Kagyu, the great scholar Pema
Pakpo from the Drukpa Kagyu, and the omniscient Takpo
Tashi Namgye. All these renowned Dakpo Kagyu masters
practiced the *Uttaratantra* teachings to actualize the meaning
of Mahamudra.

This specific lineage of Mahamudra comes from the Indian master Saraha, who taught Maitripa, one of Marpa
Lotsawa's principal teachers. Saraha's particular specialty

was action meditation practice. One day he was in a flower garden holding a skull cup filled with nectar. Glancing into the cup, he saw that all the flowers, mountains and trees were reflected in the nectar. Simply observing this phenomenon awakened his great realizations developed over many past lifetimes, and he spontaneously realized Mahamudra. He saw that all manifestations exist as a reflection of the mind, just as the trees and so forth were reflected by the nectar. This realization led to his attainment of the ultimate state and all excellent qualities. Saraha is known for his *doha* (spontaneous songs of realization) and for his text called *The Ten Suchnesses*. The lineage passed to Maitripa, and from him to Marpa and, through them, to all the great Kagyupas. After receiving teachings on *The Ten Suchnesses* from Maitripa, Marpa practiced and realized the ultimate meaning of Mahamudra, which he commemorated in a song:

> By attending the great Maitripa,
> I practiced the Mahamudra
> The meaning of which is free from all elaboration.
> In this state there are no objects to bring into the mind.

This meaning is also stated in the *Abhisamayalankara*, another text from Buddha Maitreya:

> In the mind's ultimate state
> There is nothing to bring into the mind,
> No faults or mistakes to dispel.

One merely needs to see mind's own nature directly. When one can do this successfully, it is called "perfection." The *Uttaratantra* mentions that Buddha-nature is not stained by any obscurations. The inseparable nature of all the Buddhas' qualities means that they are always present. Their nature is clear, calm, free from all obscurations; no matter what happens, it cannot be stained. This is the truth of Mahamudra.

For example, the eyes of a person with jaundice will cause him to perceive a white conch shell as yellow. This perception of a yellow shell demonstrates the relative, or samsaric, state, and the reality of the white conch shell is the absolute state. Even though the jaundiced person will see it as yellow, the shell itself has no fault to dispel. When the disease is cured, he will see the shell as it exists. Similarly, in the relative, samsaric state, all these appearances manifest through the "sickness" of ignorance. In reality, their nature is all-pervading emptiness. They are not stained in their absolute state, and we have only to purify our temporary obscurations to see this. This is the essence of Mahamudra.

This system of presenting Mahamudra by way of five aspects has a long history. The great Indian pandit Mitrazogi approached the practice and the teachings of Mahamudra in this way. The tradition was passed down to Marpa's disciple Milarepa who, in turn, taught his disciples this approach, particularly his great disciple Lekzebum. Milarepa presented Mahamudra by teaching that one generates oneself in the form of Noble Chenrezig and meditates on the fivefold aspects of the teaching. However, it was Dharma Lord Gampopa who isolated this as a distinct teaching, and the name was provided by his disciple Phagmo Drupa. Therefore, this fivefold practice should be understood to be a presentation of the entire path of Mahamudra, containing all aspects of the Buddha's teachings in five categories which are presented and practiced one after the other:

(1) The first aspect is our motivation: generation of the bodhisattva attitude;

(2) The second is generating the deity as the yidam;

(3) The third is establishment of the guru, or lama;

(4) The fourth is the actual Mahamudra (shamatha and vipashyana);

(5) The fifth is dedication.

When we speak of generating the bodhisattva attitude, there are two types: the conventional and the ultimate. The ultimate bodhisattva attitude is none other than the realization of Mahamudra itself, the ultimate state of awareness, or enlightenment. So, the first aspect of the five, the generation of the bodhisattva attitude, contains the actual Mahamudra because the ultimate bodhisattva attitude is Mahamudra.

So it is also with the second of the five, generation of the deity, or yidam. This contains Mahamudra because the yidam here is Chakrasamvara together with his consort. When one generates the yidam Chakrasamvara and his consort within oneself, one achieves the experience of the union of bliss and emptiness, thereby realizing the Mahamudra.

The third aspect of the fivefold Mahamudra is generation of the lama. The lama has four aspects, or four bodies:

(1) the manifestation body, or *nirmanakaya*, which is Lord Buddha Shakyamuni;

(2) the perfect enjoyment body, or *sambhogakaya*, which is Buddha Vairochana;

(3) the truth body, or *dharmakaya*, which is the Buddha Vajradhara; and

(4) the nature body, or *svabhavikakaya*, which is mind itself, the realization of the absolute or ultimate nature of mind, which is Mahamudra.

The fourth is the actual Mahamudra practice. This is the cultivation and perfection of shamatha and vipashyana. This first is a state of perfect mental quiescence (shamatha), whereby the full power of one-pointed mind is established. The second is the state of perfect insight (vipashyana), whereby the mind penetrates into the nature of ultimate reality. These two are joined together in the actual practice of Mahamudra.

The fifth is dedication, which is called the perfect or ultimate dedication and is associated with the Buddha Samantabhadra, wherein the one who dedicates, the object of dedication, and the dedication itself are not separated. In their ultimate nature, they are realized to be an undifferentiated unity. That non-differentiation of subject and object in the dedication is, in fact, the state of Mahamudra, the unity of all opposites and the realization of non-duality.

This fivefold Mahamudra is the common heritage of all of the schools of the Kagyu lineage. However, within this single heritage there are different commentaries, different ways of explaining all of the fine points of the fivefold Mahamudra. In particular, there are ten major commentaries. This presentation will be from the point of view of the commentaries of the Drikung Kagyu lineage. These emphasize the cultivation and practice of the fivefold Mahamudra in the context of a three-year retreat in which the Six Yogas of Naropa are practiced.

The unique quality of the Drikung Kagyu interpretation of the fivefold Mahamudra comes from Lord Jigten Sumgön. By the time he was practicing under his guru, Phagmo Drupa, he had already fulfilled the purpose of all the preliminaries— the accumulation of merit and the purification of obstacles. Having done this, he approached his teacher for the actual instructions. Lord Jigten Sumgön explained that, by the kindness of his lama, he had been able to purify his obscurations and accumulate all the merit necessary to engage in the highest practice. From that point on he wanted just one practice on which to focus rather than many different types of cultivation and meditations on various things—just one path he could follow from then on. So Phagmo Drupa gave him this fivefold Mahamudra practice, telling him that from that moment, until he attained the perfect, peerless state of Buddhahood, he need rely on nothing else but this path of fivefold Mahamudra.

So, how do we engage in this practice of fivefold Mahamudra? The practice is divided into two parts—the preliminaries and the actual practice.

1 THE PRELIMINARIES

The preliminaries are divided into three categories:

I. The outer practices, which are the common, or shared, practices;

II. The internal practices, which are uncommon, or unshared; and

III. The special, exclusive practices of Mahamudra.

I. The external, common practices of the preliminaries are fourfold:

(1) Contemplation on the difficulty of attaining the precious, fully endowed human existence;

(2) Contemplation of impermanence and death;

(3) Contemplation of karma and causality;

(4) Contemplation of the faults of cyclic existence (suffering).

These are the four external, shared, or common preliminaries.

What does it mean to say that they are "shared" or "common"? It means they are practiced in common by the three vehicles: the lesser vehicle (*Hinayana*), the great vehicle (*Mahayana*) and the secret vehicle (*Vajrayana*). All three vehicles share these four external preliminaries.

II. The four inner, or unshared, preliminary practices are:

(1) refuge;

(2) Vajrasattva practice;

(3) mandala offering; and

(4) guru yoga.

These inner preliminaries are not shared with Hinayana and Mahayana; that is, they are exclusive to Vajrayana.

III. Next are the preliminaries which are special to fivefold Mahamudra practice. There are three exclusive requirements:

(1) generating loving-kindness;

(2) generating compassion;

(3) developing the bodhisattva attitude (*bodhicitta*).

They are special, or particular, to this fivefold Mahamudra practice not because they are not found elsewhere, but because they are developed in a different way. They are used as an actual part of the preliminaries for Mahamudra so that at each stage one accumulates 100,000 repetitions of each of these practices.

Lord Phagmo Drupa taught the very special qualities of loving-kindness, compassion, and bodhicitta in the context of Mahamudra practice. He said we should look upon these three as being necessarily connected with each other. This connection can be illustrated by the example of growing a plant: Loving-kindness is like the soil into which we put the seed. Compassion is like the water and the fertilizer which we put in the soil, allowing the plant to grow. Bodhicitta is like the plant itself, like the tree of enlightenment (the bodhi tree). And so, this "bodhi tree" of the bodhisattva attitude is planted in the soil of loving-kindness and watered and fertilized with compassion. Then it grows greater and greater until it finally produces its fruit, which benefits all living beings. This fruit is the three bodies of a Buddha—two form bodies and one formless body. This, then, gives us a total of eleven preliminary practices: the four common, the four uncommon, and the three special practices.

In general, there are two necessary elements for any Vajrayana practice—the empowerment and the subsequent instructions, or commentary, for practice. These develop, ripen, and purify the continuum of the disciple just like a vessel, which is first cleansed of any defilements and then filled with the necessary fluid or substance. First you must cleanse all the defilements so that you do not adulterate or weaken whatever you place inside. That is the function of the empowerment and of the instructions for practice which are given subsequently.

The practice of Tantra has two phases—the phase of generation and the phase of accomplishment, or perfection. During the phase of generation, we generate ourselves as the deity, generate the realization, or presence, of the deity. In the phase of perfection, we actually enter into meditation on Mahamudra and perfect the realization of Mahamudra. These two phases are present with any Tantra; one generates the deity and, after having done so, one stabilizes the mind on this meditation, and gains the realization of ultimate reality. The eleven aspects of the preliminary practices, then, are completed with the generation of the bodhisattva attitude.

2 THE ACTUAL PRACTICE

After the preliminaries, one is able to go on to engage in the actual practice of Mahamudra. The first phase of the practice is meditation on the yidam; that is, the cultivation of oneself as the deity, which in this case is Chakrasamvara in consort with Vajravarahi.

It is important to understand the purpose of this practice of meditating on the yidam, or deity yoga. It is not just to imagine oneself as being this deity, but rather to completely transform one's reality. Usually, we think of ourselves as being ordinary human beings with various ideas of the world—all of our connections, all of our thoughts, all of our dichotomies—basically, immersed in the ordinary world, or samsara. Before we can attain insight into reality, that is, the practice and realization of Mahamudra, we have to get beyond this illusory reality of samsara. To do that, we generate ourselves as the deity, not just thinking of ourselves in some simple way but actually visualizing ourselves, experiencing ourselves, as the deity with the consort with all of the attributes, all of the powers, the entire environment of the deity.

When we have accomplished or cultivated our meditation to the point where we really experience ourselves in that way, then we have cut ourselves off from all of the delusions of the ordinary, samsaric world and all of the thoughts of me, mine, desire, hatred, and delusion. All of these things having to do with the ordinary world are cut off through this visualization, the accomplished visualization of oneself as the deity. Only from that point of view, being free from the ordinary world, can one then enter into the contemplation and meditation on ultimate reality, or Mahamudra. So, we free ourselves from attachment to ordinary reality by cultivating this higher, more pure, more powerful reality of the deity in the mandala, surrounded by the divine, heavenly environment possessing all the divine attributes.

Once we free ourselves from that by generating ourselves as the deity, then there is a subsequent tendency to become attached to that higher divine reality, just as we are presently attached to all of the phenomena of our ordinary self and our ordinary world. To free ourselves from that higher attachment, we have the stage of perfection, which is the direct contemplation and meditation on Mahamudra. This will free us from the divine sphere.

Following the practice of deity yoga, or meditation on the yidam, there is the meditation on the lama, or guru yoga. This practice is somewhat different here in the context of Mahamudra. Guru yoga is an important part of all Buddhist practice. The transmission of the blessings of the lineage from master to disciple is vital in all its phases. It is even more important in the practice of Vajrayana, where strictly relying on and adhering to the word of the lama is critical in order to gain the blessings of the lineage. And particularly in the Kagyu lineage, there is great emphasis on the transmission of the actual blessings, which make practice and accomplishment of practice possible. So, here we have the lineage from the great teachers of India—the great Mahasiddhas such as Saraha, Tilopa, Naropa, and all those down to the present day. In each spiritual generation the entire blessings are transmitted from master to disciple.

In the fivefold Mahamudra practice of this lineage, then, guru yoga is particularly important. In this practice, the transmission has to do with the very nature of mind itself. This realization is what is passed from the master to disciple. Above and beyond all the techniques and descriptions of practice, there is an actual transmission whereby the realization of the nature of mind from the master is planted in the disciple.

The practice of guru yoga has four sections. First is the manifestation body of the guru (nirmanakaya); second is the body of complete enjoyment (sambhogakaya); third is the truth body (dharmakaya); and fourth is the nature body (svabhavikakaya). The nirmanakaya of the guru is cultivated as, or in the form of, the Lord Buddha Shakyamuni, golden in color; the sambhogakaya is cultivated in the form of the Buddha Vairochana; the dharmakaya is cultivated in the form of the Buddha Vajradhara; and the svabhavikakaya is cultivated as Mahamudra itself, the pure and ultimate nature of mind.

The third aspect of the actual practice of Mahamudra (the first being deity yoga, the second guru yoga) is the actual meditation on Mahamudra itself, and this has two different stages:

(1) the cultivation and achievement of mental quiescence to stabilize and clarify the mind; and

(2) the cultivation and achievement of pure insight, or the highest insight into reality, using mind to penetrate into the nature of ultimate reality.

So this is the body of the meditation on Mahamudra.

The next practice, done after the practice of Mahamudra, is the conclusion consisting of the various aspects of the dedication of merit.

The practice of Mahamudra, then, is formed by the instructions of the preceptor, the lama, who shows the different ways in which to actually engage in the practice. This depends on the disciple's abilities, the sharpness of her faculties, and her diligence. The practices are described generally in terms of four levels of practitioners.

(1) *Lower Level.* This is the ordinary person who needs to be given this practice in discrete steps. First, mind is focused and stabilized until one has attained the state of shamatha, or mental quiescence. Having achieved mental quiescence, one begins to cultivate special insight, vipashyana. With mental quiescence as the basis, one develops special insight, and attains the realization of Mahamudra, of ultimate reality, of the nature of mind. This is the lowest, or ordinary, stage.

(2) *Middle Level.* This is the more highly developed, sharper, more accomplished practitioner. At this stage, the preceptor teaches how to join mental quiescence and special insight into one practice. For instance, if one were meditating on the deity Chakrasamvara, this would be a meditation on his appearance and his emptiness at the same time, conjoined into one (emptiness being the ultimate nature of the deity.) So, the appearance and ultimate nature are joined into one at this middle level of practice.

(3) *High Level.* To the very sharp, able practitioner, the preceptor gives Mahamudra practice in the form of first mastering the philosophical view of Mahamudra, then meditating on that view without engaging in other types of meditation. One goes directly to the meditation of this highest view of reality and masters that, and thereby obtains Mahamudra.

(4) *Supremely High Level.* This would be persons such as Tilopa or Naropa, those who need just a little push in order to realize the ultimate enlightenment of Mahamudra. For them, a special instruction, some key words, a special action or word will break the final barrier to the supreme realization. It is presumed that these practitioners have accomplished these other levels in former lifetimes. In this lifetime, they need only that final push in order to achieve the ultimate goal.

Two years of the three-year retreat are dedicated to this practice of fivefold Mahamudra. The other year is devoted to the Six Yogas of Naropa. In a retreat situation when one is concentrated day and night on the practice, it takes two years to investigate what we are covering now in this book. We will not attempt to go through all of the texts from Phagmo Drupa on down, but rather will offer an overview of these so as to enable us to enter into this practice and to perfect it in the future.

3   MAHAMUDRA: WHAT IS IT?

Next, to understand what is meant by Mahamudra, we will look first at the word itself and say something about its meaning. The term in Tibetan is *chak-gya chenpo*; in Sanskrit, Mahamudra. The order is reversed so that *chak-gya* means *mudra*, and *chenpo* means *maha*. First, *chak-gya* in this context refers to all phenomena without exception, everything subsumed within samsara and nirvana such that no phenomenon, nothing whatsoever, is omitted or left out. So it means the entirety of everything. *Chenpo* means great, or the highest. So this is the highest, most conclusive view which realizes all phenomena of samsara and nirvana as they actually are.

The term *mudra*, or *chak-gya*, has the commonplace meaning of a seal you would stamp on a document. Here, it signifies the seal which is "stamped" on all phenomena. It is a seal which shows validity, which testifies that something is real or valid. Therefore, the meaning is that this Mahamudra testifies to the real, or ultimate, nature of all phenomena. It is also said to be like the seal of a king under which all things of the kingdom exist. There is nothing in the kingdom which does not fall under the authority of the king. So likewise, there is nothing within samsara or nirvana which does not fall under this Mahamudra, there is no phenomenon that escapes it or exists apart from those things subsumed under Mahamudra.

The term *maha* in Mahamudra is also variously described. In one interpretation, the term *mudra* indicates quantity and the term *maha* indicates quality. The quantity here is infinite, or all-inclusive. The quality indicated by the term *maha* is understood as the highest, the most sublime.

The term *Mahamudra* is described in a commentary to the Kalachakra Tantra written by Padma Chin. There, he explains the essence of Mahamudra as being the actual Prajnaparamita; that is, the wisdom which is the source of all the Buddhas of the past, present, and future. They all arise from the Prajnaparamita, the ultimate wisdom, and that ultimate wisdom is none other than Mahamudra. In the context of Vajrayana, Mahamudra is that which unites bliss and emptiness into one, and is the ultimate realization. This occurs both through the Karma Mudra and the Wisdom Mudra. Through both of these, bliss and emptiness are united into the experience of highest enlightenment, and this is what comes together in the Mahamudra practice.

Dharma Lord Gampopa said that the *mudra* aspect of the word indicates the nature of all phenomena, including everything in samsara and nirvana, all phenomena without exception. What *mudra* means here is that all these phenomena are, in their ultimate nature, non-arising. That nature, or ultimate state, the ultimate truth of all phenomena, is referred to by this term Mahamudra. In his description, Lord Gampopa divides this term *mudra* into its two syllables, each with a meaning. The first syllable of the Tibetan term *chakgya*, *chak*, refers to the non-arising nature of all phenomena, without exception. The second syllable, *gya*, refers to the beginningless nature of this. Together, they mean "from beginningless time all phenomena are non-arising in their ultimate nature."

The term *maha* refers to the highest realization of this, and the *mudra* aspect refers to the reality itself. It is not enough that things merely exist in this ultimate way; they have always existed in this ultimate way. What we need is the realization of that nature. The state of enlightenment, or Mahamudra, is only accomplished through the realization of that ultimate nature. Just like being afraid of a piece of rope in the dark, thinking it is a snake—it is not enough that it's only a piece of rope if we think it's a snake and are terrified. We have to turn on the light and actually discover it is a piece of rope before the problem is solved.

Put another way, *maha* describes phenomena as being naturally non-arising, or naturally free of all delusory elements. If you tie a snake into a loop and toss it away, the snake will untie itself through its own knowledge or its own ability and go about its business. It doesn't need anyone to help it. So, the ultimate realization of Mahamudra can be compared to a snake by saying that it frees itself; it does not need any assistance. Mind does not need to be fixed or amended by something from the outside; rather, it frees itself. The implication of this is that all phenomena without exception are non-arising, which means that their very nature is unobstructed. They are ultimate bliss and freedom; enlightenment is their very nature. There is nothing to be added or changed to achieve the ultimate nature of things because this is what exists from the beginning.

This term *Mahamudra*, then, has all of these associations and ultimately refers to the natural state of all things as being perfect or ultimate or non-arising. All of these terms point to the fact that the nature of reality is pre-existing, or has always existed in this way. Therefore, we have many synonyms for Mahamudra—the absolute truth, emptiness, or *shunyata*, the ultimate nature of reality, the lack of inherent existence, and freedom from inherent existence.

The explanation of Mahamudra can also be divided into three:

(1) the basis;

(2) the path;

(3) the result.

(1) *Basis.* The basis, or foundation, of Mahamudra is the nature of mind itself. This is the pure, or ultimate, nature of mind, which is the same as the ultimate nature of all phenomena, completely free of inherent existence.

(2) *Path.* After accepting the basis, we cultivate the realization of that ultimate nature of all phenomena through the three phases of the path. The teachings are first acquired, then cultivated and, finally, realized. These are the three steps of Mahamudra practice—first, hearing, or studying; second, thinking, or contemplating; and third, meditating, or actualizing.

These are the teachings of Mahamudra, of the ultimate nature of all phenomena: they are like clear light, or pure emptiness, lacking even the tiniest amount of inherent existence.

(3) *Result.* Third is the result, or the fruit, of Mahamudra practice. The fruit of this process is the realization of complete non-duality so that appearances and emptiness have one taste. They are not seen as different. The conventional and ultimate are perceived simultaneously in their ultimate state of non-duality and non-differentiation, which is the highest state of realization.

4 QUESTIONS AND ANSWERS I

When you realize Mahamudra by way of deity yoga, is that realization different from the Mahamudra you realize through vipashyana?

No, they are the same as long as you accomplish the practice to the point of actually realizing the nature of mind. If it's done through deity yoga, you are doing the twofold practice of the generation stage and the perfection stage. First you're generating yourself as the deity and then you are internalizing the deity in the perfection stage. Having internalized the deity, or become one with the deity, then mind focuses on its own nature. If it realizes that nature, then Mahamudra realization is complete. Likewise, if you practice shamatha and vipashyana, you first make the mind calm, stable and focused through shamatha. On that basis, you analyze the nature of mind. If through that you realize the ultimate nature of mind, then you have realized Mahamudra. There are not two Mahamudras being realized, it's all the same goal.

What is the purpose of deity yoga? It appears that we are just substituting attachment to one illusion for another.

The basic cause of our being stuck in cyclic existence, in samsara, is our excessive attachment to various objects. It's always one object or another. To become liberated from cyclic existence, it is ultimately necessary to be free of all attachments. As for particular attachments along the way, such as attachment to the state of identifying oneself as a deity, or attachment to some type of experience that arises in meditation, or attachment to the guru—any of these things can become an obstacle if one holds on to them too long. The antidote is to practice in the overall context as prescribed. In other words, each of these has its place. Each of these is cultivated along the way for a particular purpose. As long as one keeps the goal of ultimate enlightenment in mind, then all of these will be used as tools along the way and not viewed as ultimate goals in and of themselves.

In many of the visualizations we use the term "root lama." Sometimes the root lama is identified as a particular deity and other times they say it is your personal root lama. What do we mean by "root lama?"

There are various types of root lamas, depending on the context. In receiving an empowerment you have the root lama who grants the empowerment. The lama who gives you the transmission is the root lama for the transmission. The lama who gives you the pith instructions on the recognition of the nature of your own mind is a root lama. Literally, this is called "the lama who bestows the three kindnesses," the one who gives the empowerment, transmission, and pith instructions.

Now it's possible for a person to have more than one root lama. When Marpa went to India, he had 500 lamas. His principal lamas were Naropa and Maitripa. The originator of the Shangpa Kagyu, for example, had five root lamas who were dakinis. So it's possible to have many root lamas. There is also the root lama in the context of practice. This would be the lama in whom you have great confidence and with whom you have a clear relationship of teacher and disciple. This does not necessarily involve the other categories (empowerment, etc.), but rather is the lama who imparts teachings to you and in whom you have confidence.

Another root lama would be Lord Jigten Sumgön because he made certain prophesies. He said that after he left that body (in which he was Lord Jigten Sumgön) he would return to the world. In particular, "after sixteen or seventeen generations, in times of great difficulty and problems in the world, I will return in many forms. From that time on, the practitioners may look to me as their root lama." So it's appropriate to look to Lord Jigten Sumgön as your root lama because he promised to stay in the world manifesting in various forms to guide living beings until the time when the Buddha of the future, Maitreya, manifests in this world.

How does one determine who one's personal root lama is?

The identification of the root lama is something that arises out of contact and experience with the lama. It's something which arises naturally and the signs are one's feelings toward the lama, one's feeling of connectedness. These feelings are not based on vows, are not something you make up or force, but rather they arise on the basis of previous karma, that is, from the connection with that lama in a former lifetime. So, it is something that arises in your own mind, in your own perception with regard to a lama in whom you feel an uncommon sense of trust, confidence, and inspiration.

Sometimes when people are meditating, very disturbing thoughts or feelings come up. What suggestions do you have to work with this?

This type of phenomenon is very common and is actually a good sign. It's a sign that you are mentally standing still long enough so these thoughts catch up with you. Most of the time our minds are running so fast in order to keep away from unpleasant thoughts and the things that are troubling us. Our minds go from one idea to another, always escaping the more difficult things. So when you sit in meditation, instead of creating a lot of new things, a lot of the old ones naturally arise. It's important at that time to recognize that this is in fact a sign that your mind is staying still and this is very good. Do not worry about the arising of those things, but allow them to pass also. It's necessary for the beginner to be patient and to understand that this occurs and not to be disturbed by it. Rather, one should cultivate a sense of distance from those disturbing thoughts. To be able to back off, watch them arise and anticipate that they will arise, and not be too caught up in them, that's the first step. Then when they arise, part of the mind recognizes that they are disturbing thoughts that should be cut off and can be cut off, and then proceeds to cut them off. As one develops, one gets better and more skillful at cutting them off.

Lord Jigten Sumgön had a simile for this. It's like a particular type of bird that stands right at the edge of a great river in Tibet. At a very broad and calm place, this bird looks for fish. Being very skillful, he can see the slightest ripple and indication of the fish about to surface. As soon as that fish surfaces, he's right there to scoop it up. So, that is what we cultivate in the meditation, that ability to stand back and observe the quiet flow of mind and always be ready to catch any disturbing thought or conception before it goes on and really disturbs the quiet stream of our consciousness. One method of dealing with these disturbing conceptions is to just cut them off as they arise. Another method is to let them go. Once we become more familiar with the nature of the conceptions, the reality behind them, then we become less disturbed by them and we get to the point that we don't have to cut them off. Recognizing their nature, we are not disturbed by them and we just let them be. Let them pass. They are then rendered incapable of disturbing the calmness of mind.

5 CHANNELING THE BREATH

The special practice of channeling the breath involves a meditation with three sets of three inhalations and exhalations from each nostril; that is, from each nostril separately and then with both nostrils together. Each of the three sets is the same except that its source is different. The first set is three inhalations through one nostril and three exhalations through the other; the second set is three inhalations through the second nostril and three exhalations through the first nostril; and the third set is three inhalations and exhalations using both nostrils together.

The first exhalation of each set is forceful and also very long and drawn out. The second is also forceful but it is short. The third is gentle and drawn out, natural, without any force or special exertion behind it. Do this three times from the one nostril, then repeat it with the other nostril, then once again with both.

Now, when the breathing is forceful, you don't just force it out all at once. You begin very gently, very slowly, increasing it more and more; making it very strong in the middle, and trail off with it again gently. These breaths are said to be like the quill of a porcupine. The porcupine quill is very sharp and fine at either end and big in the middle. So that's how these breaths should be—start out gently, quickly get stronger and stronger, and then trail off. The reason for this is that there are many very small, fine channels for the breath. Rather than strain them all at once, which wouldn't be effective, you follow their subtlety by starting off gently so they will open up. If you force the breath out all at once there is a danger that they will not open or that these fine, subtle channels could be harmed. As you inhale, your lungs fill up completely. Once they are completely filled, pause, and then do the exhalation.

As you inhale, you visualize all of the Buddhas of the three times in the ten directions sending their blessings in the form of rays of light. As you inhale, you are taking in all of these rays of blessings till you are completely filled with them. As you exhale, you breathe out the darkness of all of the defilements accumulated over many lifetimes from beginningless time. You breathe these out completely.

Now the breathing, the inhalation and exhalation, should be from very deep, from the bottom of the diaphragm so that you're filling your lungs completely. Then you expel it from the top down. At the end, the lower diaphragm forces out the last of the air.

To close the nostrils, hold your thumb at the base of your third finger. That blocks the channel through which harmful forces or destructive demons would enter. With your thumb at the base of that finger, extend your forefinger and fold your other three fingers over the thumb. Use the forefinger to block the opening of the nostril. Don't push the side of your nostril, but rather block the opening of the nostril from below.

This is recommended for when you first get up in the morning before you say any other prayers or do any other meditation. At least one complete sequence should be done; two sequences is very good.

First set

1. Block the left nostril,
    inhale slowly and deeply through the right nostril.
   Block the right nostril,
    exhale long and hard through the left nostril.
2. Block the left nostril,
    inhale slowly and deeply through the right nostril.
   Block the right nostril,
    exhale short and hard through the left nostril.
3. Block the left nostril,
    inhale slowly and deeply through the right nostril.
   Block the right nostril,
    exhale long and gently through the left nostril.

Second set

1. Block the right nostril,
    inhale slowly and deeply through the left nostril.
   Block the left nostril,
    exhale long and hard through the right nostril.
2. Block the right nostril,
    inhale slowly and deeply through the left nostril.
   Block the left nostril,
    exhale short and hard through the right nostril.
3. Block the right nostril,
    inhale slowly and deeply through the left nostril.
   Block the left nostril,
    exhale long and gently through the right nostril.

Third set

1. Without blocking,
    inhale slowly and deeply.
   Without blocking,
    exhale long and hard.
2. Without blocking,
    inhale slowly and deeply.
   Without blocking,
    exhale short and hard.
3. Without blocking,
    inhale slowly and deeply.
   Without blocking,
    exhale long and gently.

6 BODY POSTURE

Generally, the focus of teachings on Mahamudra and other dharmas is on the disposition of mind; that is, what to do with mind, how to focus mind, how to analyze phenomena, and so forth. Very little discussion is centered on the disposition of the body; however, this is very important. You will find in descriptions of practices like the Six Yogas of Naropa that there is significant discussion of this, although it doesn't take as much space as the discussion of mind. So, it is very important to know what to do with the body while engaging in various types of meditation.

First, there is the teaching on the sevenfold posture of Buddha Vairochana. The first of the seven aspects is the placement of the legs. In this posture, the legs are crossed in the lotus position, also called the vajra position. This position has many benefits. The benefit discussed in this context is that of redirecting one of the five winds. There are five main winds in the body. One is called the downward-clearing wind. Normally this wind is involved in all of the processes of evacuating things from the body, like the bowels, the urine, and so forth. It is responsible for anything that is pushed downward and out the lower orifices.

Regarding its function for the mind, it is engaged in the activity of the *kleshas* (poisons): greed, hatred, ignorance, jealousy, and pride. Of these five, the downward-clearing wind is most connected with the klesha of jealousy. Placing the legs in the vajra position inhibits, or blocks, the function of jealousy and in general redirects the force of the downward-clearing wind to the central channel, thereby clarifying mind and inhibiting the klesha of jealousy.

Next, the hands are folded together, palm upward, right on top of the left. The thumbs are held over the palms. The position of the right palm should be four finger-widths below the navel. This hand position redirects the force of the wind which is associated with the water element. By inhibiting its movement, by redirecting it to the central channel, the klesha of anger is inhibited.

Next, the spine is set very straight, not leaning one way or the other, forward or back, but completely straight up and down. You should visualize it as a stack of coins one on top of the other, all the way up the length of the spine such that it would fall over if it leaned one way or the other. The shoulders should be held back a bit, opening up the chest. This is said to be like a soaring bird with its wings stretched back, but don't hold them too far back, just a little. Another way to think of this posture is that you are holding your chest outward and shoulders slightly back. This causes the wind associated with the earth element to enter the central channel, thereby inhibiting the klesha of delusion.

The chin is held slightly downward and the tongue is held up towards the palate near the base of the upper front teeth. The teeth are held slightly open so air can pass between the upper and lower teeth, so don't clench the jaw. All of this influences the wind associated with the fire element, causing it to enter the central channel and inhibit the klesha of desire.

The eyes should be generally directed at a spot four finger-widths in front of the tip of the nose and slightly downward. Gently, softly focus at that spot about an arm's length in front of your nose. The eyes should not be wide open, just gently look in that direction. This influences the wind associated with the space element, causing it to enter the central channel and inhibit the klesha of pride.

This position of the body is very important because the channels within the body will follow the external disposition of the body. The way the body is placed will set the channels; and the winds, of course, flow inside the channels, so if they are properly set, the winds will flow properly. Mind follows the wind. To focus the mind properly, the winds must also be functioning properly.

The closest association between the mind and the winds comes through the eyes. The focus, or disposition, of the eyes is influenced by the winds, which in turn influence mind, so it is very important how the eyes are focused. For the beginner, it's easiest for the gaze to be directed somewhat downward and in front of you. A more advanced practice takes place with the eyes focused more straight ahead, and some highly advanced practices involve looking somewhat upward. There is also an association between the various practices and various goals or attainments. The manifestation body, nirmanakaya, is associated with the gaze directed downward, sambhogakaya straight ahead, and dharmakaya with the gaze directed slightly upward. The direction and focus of the eyes is important depending on one's disposition and the relative predominance of the elements.

The four elements are of different strengths in different individuals. Some individuals are said to have a relatively greater amount of the earth element, for instance. Such a person will tend to relax and easily fall asleep, get drowsy very easily. For that type of person, it's good to focus the eyes somewhat upward which will help keep them from falling into lethargy and sleep. Others, whose minds are constantly disturbed by random thoughts or excited thoughts, should look downward to help gain control over that process.

Following the gradual, or the ordered, course of the teachings, after the disposition of the body come the discussions of shamatha and vipashyana.

Aspect of Posture	Energy Redirected to the Central Channel	Afflicting Emotion Inhibited
Legs folded in lotus position	Downward clearing wind	Jealousy
Hands placed right over left and held four finger-widths below the navel	Wind associated with the water element	Anger
Straight spine	Wind associated with the earth element	Delusion
Chin down, tongue against the palate, and jaw relaxed	Wind associated with the fire element	Desire
Eyes set downward	Wind associated with the space element	Pride

7 SHAMATHA: STABILIZING THE MIND

In this text, shamatha and vipashyana are discussed in order of their cultivation. First there will be a discussion of how to cultivate shamatha. Once that is mastered, you go on to cultivate vipashyana.

Shamatha is the Sanskrit term; *shinay* is the Tibetan. What is the meaning of these words? *Shinay* has two syllables, each with a meaning. *Shi* comes from the word *shiwa*, which means to pacify. *Nay* means to abide, or to stay. What is being pacified here is the tendency of mind to act in an uncontrolled, wild manner, to go this way and that. Of course, all things follow the mind. To gain control of mind is of primary importance in the practice of meditation and the practice of Dharma in general. So first we gain control of mind, pacify it, then stabilize it—that's what *nay* means. So the mind is stabilized in this state of pacification, or control, called *shinay*. In English, one could say "mental quiescence."

There are two general types of mental quiescence meditation. The first has an object of, or support for, meditative focus. The second is meditation without an object of meditative focus.

"Support" refers to an actual object, a visual object, so it is called "meditation which has an object." Any type of physical object could be used for focus. It can be made of wood or stone or even be a spot on the rug or wall. The physical object in this type of mediation should not be something very bright or very light in color. Something subdued or in a darker color is better. If it's too light, the object can strain the eyes and cause them to tear. The focus should be with the eyes half closed, not wide open, not shut. It should be something one can look at comfortably without blinking very much. Too much blinking causes one's mind to lose its focus.

In this shamatha, or mental quiescence, meditation, it's very important to understand that you are seeking to cut off the *kalpana* (in Tibetan, *tok ba*). Kalpana are any type of thoughts, any type of concepts. Technically, they are called dichotomizing thoughts, something which creates a division between one thing and another, usually between oneself and another thing. All such conceptual mental functions are to be cut off. This mental quiescence meditation is just simple awareness, focused and calm, on an object. As thoughts and concepts arise, they should be abandoned, cut off—never taken up or followed.

With regard to the object, there are two dangers—one, that mind will go out to the object and, the other, that mind will take the object in. If you choose an object, for example a stone, and meditate on it, you may start to notice that the stone has very interesting lines on it. You find that the colors of the stone are very pleasing. Then your mind has gone out to the object, into thoughts about the object, and you have lost your concentration. One must avoid these thoughts about the object. If one's mind starts getting distracted by the object itself, thinking about the qualities, the color, the position, the workmanship, all of these things, this is no good. It has to be a mere awareness of the object whereby the object is taken as a whole and not analyzed or evaluated. Just focus on it, purely and simply.

Attention can also turn inward, so that you're really not focusing on the object at all. You're just thinking, "Oh, I have this object which is a stone, and I'm meditating on it, and I'm cultivating this shamatha meditation." This is called taking the object inward; it occurs when you are thinking more about yourself or about the process. This is incorrect meditation because it is just a kalpana, a mental process which causes a dichotomy between oneself and the object. Likewise, any thoughts that are analytical, such as, "Am I the same as the stone or am I different? Is my mind the same as the stone or different? Is the stone in my mind or is my mind in the stone?" are just more kalpana which should be cut off.

There are many strategies one can adopt regarding the object of meditative focus. In different teachings, different objects are mentioned, things like a butter lamp or a candle. These are okay, but there is no need to be concerned about the type of object. The point of this type of meditation is to train the mind to hold one object single-pointedly and undistractedly, to gain the power of one-pointed concentration which excludes all the kalpana. It doesn't matter so much what the object is, so long as you avoid an object that will distract your mind by its very nature.

If one is involved in the generation stage of tantric practice, then it's good to use the yidam as the object of focus—but only if one can do so without being distracted by it. Evaluating it and thinking about it so much that concepts arise will cause you to lose meditative focus. One should take in the yidam, the image of Buddha, without thinking about it. Take in the whole image just as it is, without focusing on one part of it to the exclusion of others. That way, you're really doing more than one thing at once. You're not simply cultivating mental quiescence, you are also gaining proximity, or connectedness, with the tantric yidam. This can be very helpful to the process of the generation stage, but you should always remember that the cultivation of mental quiescence does not depend on which object you choose. It is a process of training the mind to focus single-pointedly on any object.

We have explained the meditation with a visual support. The next step is the development of mental quiescence without a visual support. This, too, is divided into two categories. The first is the meditation which cultivates mental quiescence by focusing on breathing.

Breathing is not a visual support; however, it is an object of focus. As before, the point is to avoid all dichotomizing thoughts, all kalpanas, and focus merely on the breath, on the flow of the breath outward and inward. It's important to be careful to not allow thoughts to arise, even about the object. For instance, focusing on the sensation around the nostrils that comes from the movement of the air is fine. But, it's important not to allow this to give rise to thoughts such as, "Now the breath is leaving, now the breath in coming back in." These are conceptual thoughts. So, it should be simply a focusing on the actual breath itself.

Lord Jigten Sumgön said that this type of meditation, focusing on the breath, can lead to a very powerful state of one-pointed concentration called the vajra-like samadhi. He said this is true because this type of meditative focus can easily, or expediently, free mind from all conceptual thought, making it an extremely powerful type of meditation.

So, there are these two varieties of focusing meditation without visual support—the first is with a physical support, the breath. The second is without even a focus on the breath. It is a focusing meditation which allows mind to stay focused without any type of visual or physical object. In this type of meditation, the aim is to cut off any thoughts or conceptions, kalpana, that arise. Immediately cut them off and let the mind return to the focused state without any support or object.

The next discussion concerns what is called "meditation without signs." This is about the nature of the meditation itself, rather than about the focus, or "sign," of the meditation. Here, one can find that there are two different tendencies or two different extremes. One is too tight and the other is too loose. When concentration is too loose, it is necessary to tighten it up, and when it's too tight, one must loosen it.

Sensory objects, such as auditory stimulation, can distract the mind and cause it to lose focus and become very loose, or lax. Even when one is sitting in a focused meditation cultivating mental quiescence, hearing a sound or seeing something can disturb the mind. If that occurs, it's necessary to cut it off and return your attention to mind itself. In this case, it is not so much the kalpana which are to be cut off, but rather one's reaction to a sensory object.

Next are the flaws associated with laxity and tightness in meditation. We are not necessarily referring to a physical laxity. The body might be held in a very proper posture, but internal laxity may arise anyway. This is said to be like a softness inside, a sort of relaxation whereby mind wanders in a more subtle way, rather than in the gross way of thinking about different kalpana as discussed before. This is a very subtle conceptualization which does not take the form of actual thoughts, but rather is associated with the sensation of internal relaxation. One can get caught up in it without conceptualizing. This fault disturbs one-pointed mental focus.

Just as the mind can become relaxed while in the proper posture and subtle interferences or conceptualizations can arise, likewise subtle disturbances take place when the mind is held too tightly. In other words, if mind is held too alertly, too strenuously, then, even if the gross conceptions do not arise, subtle ones do and a subtle disturbance of the mind takes place. So, the practice of mental quiescence, or shamatha, meditation depends upon this near-perfect balance of tightness and laxity of mind.

The correct balance can be compared to spinning thread from cotton. There, it is very important not to make it too tight or the string will break; if it is too loose, the thread will not be formed properly. Another example is someone playing a stringed instrument. To get the right tone, the string mustn't be too tight or too loose, it has to be right in between. Concentration is critical in keeping mind in this proper aspect of not being strained too much, not trying too hard to keep the focus, and not letting the focus become too relaxed.

At the beginning, this is not going to come naturally. One should expect to spend a great amount of effort in keeping mind focused in this balanced way. Because of this, the beginner is always advised to keep meditation sessions very brief. Six minutes is about the proper time for a meditative session. Then you should take a break, and again enter into the meditation. You can do that ten times (that would be ten six-minute sessions, with a break between each one.) Otherwise, if you try to hold it too long in the beginning, these subtle and gross forms of distraction are inevitable. It's not good to force it and remain meditating even though your mind is overcome with these distractions.

This, then, is a brief description of mental quiescence, or shamatha, meditation.

8 VIPASHYANA: ANALYZING THE NATURE OF MIND

Next is the process of cultivating vipashyana, or the perfect insight that leads us to a knowledge of ultimate reality by focusing on and analyzing mind itself. This is part of what is done in the three-year retreat. In order to practice this, one looks at mind itself. In order to focus on mind, one needs mental quiescence so that the mind is controlled and focused one-pointedly, not distracted by various conceptions. It is also very helpful to be in a proper place. This is the importance of retreat, where one is free from everyday distractions and can focus on the nature of mind in a calm and open way.

Dharma Lord Gampopa taught that the way we should approach vipashyana meditation is to look at mind itself and analyze it, trying to understand what it is, what its defining characteristics are, and so forth. He spoke of different ways investigating mind:

First of all, what is the substance, the entity, of mind?

Second, what is its nature?

Third, what are its defining characteristics?

Of these, first is the essential substance of mind. When we look at mind, the first essential substance, or entity, we find is clarity. We find that mind itself is free of conceptualization.

Next we look at the nature of mind. Dharma Lord Gampopa said, "The nature of mind is free from the three attributes of generation, annihilation, and abiding." Third, the defining characteristic of its aspect, its appearance, is that it arises at all times. Whether in samsara or nirvana, there is always the arising of mind.

The essence of mind is somewhat difficult to explain, so we look at it from the negative point of view, that is, what mind is not. First of all, we see that it is not something which arises or ceases or abides. It is free of these three things. From beginningless time, there is no arising, no cessation and no abiding in terms of staying in one place, not moving, or not changing. It is completely free of all three of these.

It is also free of being a thing or a substance composed of particles. The essential entity, or substance, of mind is not something that can be defiled or stained by grasping at subject and object. It is completely free of the stains from those activities.

Further, when we look at the essential substance of mind, we find that no matter how much we search for it, no matter how much we analyze it, there is no *thing* there to be found. There is no entity that we can come up with by searching, evaluating, and analyzing. No matter how much we seek for its essential substance, we cannot find it. The searcher, the one who does the search for the essential substance of mind, cannot find it. Therefore it is said that the essential substance of mind itself is emptiness.

Mind is that which cannot be isolated or located or defined through logical analysis. All phenomena exist conventionally, but when subjected to an analysis which seeks to find their essential substance, one cannot be found. That is their ultimate reality.

So here we have the distinction between conventional reality and ultimate reality. All phenomena, including mind, exist conventionally, but when we search for what they actually are we find nothing. That is their emptiness, or ultimate reality. The nature of mind, then, is not different in this sense from the nature of all phenomena in samsara and nirvana.

That is, when all phenomena are subjected to conclusive analysis of their essential substance, nothing is found. Therefore, they are said to be "empty," or to lack inherent identifiability, or inherent substance.

If even one thing were found to possess an inherent nature, then this could establish a basis for other things to possess an inherent nature or identifiability, but this is not the case. Therefore, the emptiness of all things is the same; all things in samsara and nirvana—all phenomena—are empty of this inherent nature. This is what Aryadeva said in his *Madhyamika Shadashadika*: "The substance of one thing is the substance of all things. The emptiness of one thing is the same as the emptiness of all things." This means that the lack of inherent nature is all-pervasive, just as the basic nature of all things is their emptiness. That is their ultimate reality.

No distinction can be made between those things which have inherent existence and those which do not because there is nothing whatsoever which possesses inherent existence. This ultimate nature of all phenomena is what is realized through the practice of vipashyana, the cultivation of perfect insight. This refers to perfect insight into the nature of reality generated by looking at mind itself. One analyzes mind and all phenomena by seeking for their essential substance, their true nature and their defining characteristics, and by doing so, one finds that they are empty of these things. From that, one becomes released from these illusions.

However, it is very important that this not be merely an intellectual exercise of learning to say that all things lack inherent existence. That is very easy to do, but it does not help. It is necessary that this realization become an immediate one from the deepest place of mind. We are to look at the way mind responds to phenomena. It responds not according to intellectual understanding, but according to the way it really sees things, the way it understands things in the deepest way.

So the process of meditation here enables us to take the superficial intellectual understanding and internalize it, make it so we actually realize things in this way. The only way that can be done is by doing it ourselves—personally taking all these steps to the realization of the nature of mind and all phenomena. This is done through a process of analysis in which we question all our assumptions about conventional phenomena. We investigate and analyze conventional phenomena starting with mind and continue in this way until we destroy all of our preconceptions and look directly upon these objects themselves. When we realize their emptiness, it is our own realization and at that point it is of great benefit to us.

Here, the text on the cultivation of perfect insight presents a dialectical question-and-answer between a challenger and a defender. The former continually challenges assumptions about the nature of mind by asking penetrating questions. The answers, the defense, we must come up with ourselves. Our meditation, then, is to use these questions to focus on our deeply held assumptions of what mind is, who we are, and what reality is. By using them in this way, we can penetrate this subject and come up with our own direct realization of the answers.

This analysis focuses in two different directions—on the subject and on the object. *Subject* in "focusing on the subject" refers to the one who is doing the analysis, the one who is doing the meditation, the one who is holding the assumptions, the one who is striving for the realization. By looking at and analyzing the subject, one realizes what is called selflessness of the person. *Object* in "focusing on the object" refers to all the things that the subject holds on to, the outer world. What is realized here is the selflessness of phenomena. These, then, are the two forms of selflessness. They are also called the two forms of emptiness, the emptiness of persons, and the emptiness of phenomena.

Put another way, this analysis is meant to determine the nature of mind itself and the nature of the mind's contents. Contents refers to the objects: those things that are perceived or held by mind through the sense powers. By looking at them, we can determine the nature of the contents of mind. So, mind and its contents are the ultimate focus of this meditation.

In order to focus attention on the nature of mind, one must first set oneself in the state of mental quiescence. Only after having calmed and clarified the mind and made it one-pointed can one begin the practice of vipashyana. So, the first step here is to enter into a state of quiescence and then raise the questions, "What is it that is quiescent? What is it that is abiding? Is it the body or is it mind?" The body is very easy to observe, so it's clear that this is not what we are concerned with here; rather it is with mind itself.

If we conclude, "Well, it is mind which is quiescent now, mind which is abiding," then these next questions naturally arise. If mind is staying still, if it's quiescent, then it must have some form, some shape, some color. There must be something there that we can find or identify. If there is something there, then it must have a shape. Is it square, is it round, is it shaped like a pyramid? What is its size—large or small? What is its color? These are all attributes of things which exist, so we must look for something like them. For something to exist, it must have some attribute which qualifies its existence, something that allows us to say that it exists. If there is something there, it must have a size, a shape, a color; it must have some attribute.

If something exists, then it must have a location. So next we look for the location of mind. We ask the questions, and analyze whether it is inside the body or outside the body. Is it partly inside and partly outside? Where exactly does it exist? Where does it abide? Next, does it abide in the object? If we look and see a flower, is mind in the flower or is mind going out to the flower and coming back? When we hear a sound, is it mind going out grasping the sound? Is mind out where the sound is? Is mind part of the sense powers? Exactly where does the mind function?

If we decide that mind abides in the body somewhere, then we look for it in the body. Is it in one specific place in the body or does it circulate around in the body like the blood? If we look at the different parts of the body, like the internal organs or the limbs, we see that we have sensation, or awareness. Mind may seem to be in one place, but not always. Is it moving about? Is it in one certain organ of the body like the heart, kidney, or spleen, or is it in different organs, or in all of the parts of the body?

In this analytical meditation we must be very specific and precise, understanding that imprecision or just assuming something to be true is a source of great error. We have to really make a decision, really be very specific and very careful. Western science and medicine tend to assume that mind is located in the brain. If we accept that assumption and look at the brain itself, we see that it has many parts. Where does mind exist in these many parts? Does it exist in some and not others? In a specific one or in all of them? We analyze very minutely in this way.

Then, we look at the mind's movement. Mind seems to move, so where does it arise? Where does it stay for awhile? Where does it go next? We look at things like our thoughts and perceptions. Where do they come from, where are they located, where do they stay while they exist, and where do they go next? We can extend that questioning to mind itself. Where does it arise in the body, where does it stay, and where does it go at the time of death? Does it stay behind in the body, or does it go somewhere else? What is the nature of its existence in these different ways? We try to actually pin it down and define it. We must exert ourselves very methodically, systematically examining all of these assumptions about the nature of the existence of mind.

Up to this point in our investigation of the nature of mind, we have been looking at where mind exists. In doing so, we focused somewhat outwardly, as if we were looking for an object which exists somewhere and were trying to find out where. Having exhausted that line of inquiry, we next turn inward and look at the searcher.

So, we extend the search with a requirement, or demand, that the search prove fruitful, either positively or negatively. That a determination be made is the key. When we make this search, we cannot just leave the investigation hanging but we require ourselves to come to a conclusion. If we find something, that is all well and good, but if we don't, that's fine too. However, one way or the other we must pursue the search until we make a determination.

KALPANA

In going about this search, various types of kalpana arise. The kalpana, again, are the whole range of conceptual thoughts which conceive of objects and subjects, or make any sort of dualistic assumptions. We have already seen these kalpana in the process of stabilizing meditation. When we try to focus one-pointedly on an object, sometimes these kalpana arise, that is, we start thinking about something, and some conception arises. So next we look at those kalpana and try to find out something about them. What are they like? What is their origin ? Where do they abide? Where do they go? What are their various characteristics?

At this point we analyze them very minutely. If they exist in fact (and they clearly exist in some way), from what do they arise? They seem to arise like sprouts suddenly coming forth out of the ground. So we look at the ground out of which they arose, which seems to be mind. So if they arose out of mind, are they the same as mind or are they different? Are they mind itself? Are they some content of mind? How do they arise? What are they made of? How do they relate to mind itself?

There are certain possibilities here when we analyze mind and the kalpana. First of all, it seems reasonable to say that the thoughts, the kalpana, arise in mind. If they arise from mind, the next question is, do they arise simultaneously with mind? In other words are they of the very substance of mind? The analogy used here is the relationship between the sun and sunlight. Sunlight arises from the sun, and it seems to be of the same essence as the sun. However, the sun is there and the sunlight is here, so there is some question. If we say the kalpana relate to mind like sunlight relates to the sun, then they always go together. You don't have sunlight without the sun, nor do you have sun without sunlight. They arise together, exist together; wherever there is one there is the other. In this sense, they are inseparable and arise at the same time. So, if we say that mind and kalpana are like that, then we are saying that wherever there are kalpana there is mind and wherever there is mind there are kalpana. In that way, we analyze until we come to a conclusion, a determination.

If that's not quite right, then we try another possibility. We say maybe the kalpana arise only in the presence of certain contributing conditions. Maybe they are not always found wherever there is mind. We can say this case is like a stick of incense and its smoke: mind being like the stick of incense and kalpana being like the smoke. Often they are found together, but they are not necessarily together. It takes a contributing condition for smoke to arise from the incense, and that contributing condition is fire. If you remove or extinguish the fire in the incense, then the smoke will no longer arise. Likewise, if the incense is exhausted, then no smoke arises, even if there is plenty of fire. In this case, the relationship between the two is dependent upon contributing conditions. So we analyze mind and see whether there is some type of contributing condition that causes the kalpana to arise from mind and without which they do not arise.

It is helpful to look at different analogies that illustrate the possible relationships between mind and its conceptual contents. Another example is a mirror and the reflections in the mirror, which are clearly of a different nature. The images are not inherent in the mirror, but they arise in the mirror whenever a contributing condition is there, the contributing condition being some visible object in the proximity of the mirror. If an object is there, then it will be reflected in the mirror; if it's not, it won't be reflected. In addition, even if that object is reflected in the mirror; the reflection is there only from one angle. If you move to another angle and look at that same mirror you won't see that object reflected in it. So it depends not only on the presence of the object but on the angle of viewing, one's perspective.

So perhaps mind and kalpana are like that—the kalpana only appear in mind when some object, some stimulation, is in some proximity of mind. And even then, the kalpana only appear in mind from a certain perspective. If you look at mind in the same moment from a different perspective, perhaps the kalpana would not even appear.

Yet another example is that of the moon being reflected in water. When the moon is shining in the sky and you have a pool of water, you can see a reflection of the moon in that water. The reflection is like kalpana. If you take ten or twelve bowls, and fill them all with water, then you will see that one moon reflected ten or twelve times, depending upon the number of pools of water you have and where you're standing. So the question is, are mind and the kalpana like that? Can you have one stimulus and many kalpana? Here, the water is like mind—if you have several pools of water then you can have many images of the moon simultaneously. If you have one stimulus or object, can many kalpana arise simultaneously? This would be like having some object and there arising in mind the thought that "Oh, this is beautiful" and other thoughts arising from that very same stimulus such as, "This is good," "This is large," and so forth.

All the different types of concepts which can arise with regard to a stimulus—certainly they can arise in mind, but can they, like the moon being reflected in multiple pools of water, arise simultaneously? That is a key question. Is the function of mind like the pools of water, which can contain discrete images? This doesn't seem to be the case. Usually, if we feel that something is good, then that concept, that kalpana, pulls our attention. Immediately, we can say, "Oh no, it's bad," but that is subsequent, not simultaneous. The theory that the mind has many thoughts at once is problematic.

Another analogy which serves as a basis for analysis is that mind and the kalpana are related like a mother and child; the mother represents mind and the child is the kalpana. So we could say that the kalpana are born to mind like a child is born to a mother. If the relationship is like that, then we can look at various possibilities. Once the child is born, the mother and child can both exist together. Once the kalpana are produced by mind, can they exist together? What if the child dies and the mother lives? Can the mind continue while the kalpana are cut off or lost? There is another possibility: that the child lives and the mother dies. In this case, you would have no more mind, but the kalpana would continue. This is another possibility that must be analyzed and tested for validity.

Next it should be determined how the mind and kalpana relate in terms of their movement. If they are the same thing, are they the same in essence? There appears to be a difference. Is this appearance of difference a true one or is it not? This must be determined. In other words, does mind project the kalpana? Are they something produced and projected outward? Or, on the other hand, do the kalpana really arise from something out there and come into mind? Are the kalpana a function of mind, like an activity in which mind engages? These things should be determined very clearly to understand the nature of mind and its contents.

This, then, is the first of four categories of investigation, that is, looking at mind in terms of the kalpana, the thought patterns that arise in mind, what they are, and how they interrelate with one another.

OBJECTS OF AWARENESS

In this practice, we focus on what are generally assumed to be external objects in the environment. These are like the types of objects that were used in the beginning stages to cultivate mental quiescence. They could be any object of mind, anything which we perceive, any object which we take to be existent in our environment. For instance, we could take a glass of water on the table and ask, Is this a projection of my mind? Does it exist externally? What is the relationship between this glass and my mind? Are they of the same essence or are they of different essences? These questions must be pursued until one gains a clear, direct realization that answers the questions and removes all doubt.

Here we ask very difficult questions about the relationship between mind and these objects. First of all, if the object and mind are of the same essence, then what is the function or the mechanism which makes it seem to be external? Is it projected out of mind? Does it exist within mind and is projected so as to appear outside? Is the nature of mind outside, so that the projection is inward and we only think that mind is in here perceiving something out there? If it is not of the same essence of mind and exists as a free, independent entity external to mind, then what is the mechanism which allows it to appear in mind or arise as an object of mind? This investigation becomes very subtle when we look into the nature of the possibilities of external objects appearing to mind. Is this a case of projection from one side, projection from the other side, or a case of no projection, and if so, how is the contact possible?

MOVEMENT OF MIND

Third, we investigate whether mind is something which abides and exists in one spot, or whether it is something that goes out and moves around from one thing to another. Now, we can see that when we cultivate mental quiescence, mind becomes focused one-pointedly on its object. It does not waver from that object and abides stably over a period of time on that object. So at that time, it would appear that mind is unmoving and stable.

However, when we practice vipashyana, in which we cultivate perfect insight, mind is going from one object to another, it's moving around to objects nearby and far away. So here it seems most clear that mind is moving a great deal. What we have to determine at this point is how mind can do both. What is the nature of mind such that it seems to move around but is sometimes stable? Or is it actually stable and this movement is an illusion? At this point we focus more and more on mind and its functions, particularly its movement.

If we assume that mind itself is still and that it's just the contents that seem to be moving, then we focus on the mind and look for an explanation. If we assume that mind is a very dynamic thing that never stays still, then we can investigate to see how it can become perfectly still and stable. So, we look more and more minutely into these subtle changes from one moment to the next in the contents and the function of mind. We ask all these questions and analyze mind and look for things like the arising of the kalpana to see whether they are produced. If they are produced, do they abide? If they abide, do they disappear? Are they destroyed? When we investigate this, we cannot find any point of birth or arising nor any point of destruction, and yet there is the impression that they are coming into existence and passing out again.

ESSENTIAL NATURE OF MIND

So, from here we observe more carefully the essential nature of mind. Mind has the quality of clarity, which seems to be a defining characteristic. Another defining characteristic is its emptiness. Mind has an emptiness like space which can contain things like the kalpana. So, is mind then clarity, or is it emptiness? Is it some combination of these two?

When we initially hear these questions, we can arrive at some sort of an understanding of the purpose of asking them. We can form some preliminary determinations about some of them: which way we would think things actually exist and, through that, arrive at some level of understanding. But we should remind ourselves that understanding, simply understanding, is not what we are aiming at. Mere understanding is not adequate to overcome these very basic and long-held assumptions about the nature of mind and reality. What we need is an absolutely firm, unhesitating determination that arises only out of direct realization of the truth revealed through these questions.

In order to achieve this, we need to set about this process in a very systematic and thorough way, one that is characterized by great diligence and hard work. That is why it is preceded by the development of mental quiescence. It is practiced in a condition of isolation in which one removes oneself from all of the concerns and busyness of the world and goes off into a retreat where these questions can be investigated thoroughly without distraction. Then, if we really work at each point for maybe a week or so, we can arrive at some clear determination and understand in the most profound way what the answer is. It is only this most profound understanding, or realization, that has the ability to bring about the transformation that is the goal of the practice.

9 MEDITATION EXERCISES AND INSTRUCTIONS

Visualize all things in the form of the syllable *HUNG* while chanting the syllable. Whatever arises, whether internal or external, becomes *HUNG*. All thoughts become *HUNG*. All things become *HUNG*; a small stone becomes a little *HUNG*, a big tree becomes a big *HUNG*. When we practice chanting *HUNG*, we do so by making the sound in our mouths without closing our teeth. There should always be a space there. In this practice three things are united in this syllable *HUNG*: the wind (dynamic internal energies), consciousness, and appearances. Do this practice for approximately ten minutes.

HUNG

Chant the syllable *HUNG* while doing the following visualization. Visualize the entire universe, both near and far off, all elements of it, in the form of the syllable *HUNG*. Imagine the large objects as being large *HUNGs*, the small, tiny ones as tiny *HUNGs*. Visualize all of these syllables coming from every corner of the universe and entering into your body through the doors of the senses. As they enter the body, they transform all of one's internal elements into the syllable *HUNG*. Again, their sizes depend upon the element and the size of the element they replace, until the entire body is filled with nothing but the syllable *HUNG*. Do this exercise for approximately ten minutes.

Here is another way in which to chant the syllable *HUNG*. Say it very strongly, very quickly, and very powerfully. As you say it, the syllables within us go outward, radiating out from our center in all directions. Each syllable projects out in all directions like bullets being sprayed by a machine gun, going extremely fast, extremely powerfully. Each one is like a bullet that is so strong and fast that it penetrates through everything. Nothing can obstruct it, not trees, rocks, not even mountains. Nothing can oppose it. The syllable *HUNG* in all its forms and all its sizes within us, radiates outward in all directions like this. Visualize it going out with nothing obstructing it. Practice this method for approximately ten minutes.

Now meditate on just one syllable *HUNG* in the space in front of you, or if you prefer, in your heart or throat or head. If you prefer having the actual shape there in front of you, you can set out a book or page with the syllable *HUNG* on it and just look at that. In any case, meditate on just this one syllable with your eyes open or closed, however you like. Let your mind relax into the syllable. Practice this for approximately ten minutes.

Now meditate on breathing. Here, it is important to keep in mind that your awareness should be only on the breathing, on merely watching the flow of the breath out of the nose and back in. One's awareness can be focused somewhere in the area right in front of the nose so as to experience the flow of the breath inward and outward. It is important not to think about it, not to conceptualize it, not to think, "Now the breath is flowing out. Now the breath is flowing in." Rather, merely observe it. Practice this for approximately ten minutes.

Now focus on just relaxing your body from the inside so that the entire area inside your chest is very relaxed and comfortable. Especially the area around the navel should be very relaxed and open. Practice this silent meditation for approximately ten minutes.

In all the various types of meditation, there are certain problems that generally arise when you meditate. These problems can be summed up into two tendencies which harm one's meditation:

(1) A sinking of mind, which is associated with drowsiness and lethargy. Mind and the attention sink, sort of collapse, or fall inward, so that one becomes drowsy.

(2) A scattering tendency where one's attention goes this way and that to all sorts of different things, so that one becomes highly distracted.

These are the two tendencies which must be dealt with in the process of meditation.

With the sinking of mind, you feel heavy and sort of fuzzy, focus falls into the center, you become tired, your eyes start to close, and you lose the object of your meditation. The antidote is to open the doors of the senses, for example, open the eyes a bit further. When mind sinks the eyelids begin to get heavy and the eyes tend to close more and more. It is as if the eyes were focusing in a more inward than outward direction. So the antidote is to open the eyes more, almost like you are trying to extend your eyeballs. You're pushing energy outward and opening your eyes rather than letting it all come inward and the eyes close.

You do the same with the other sense powers, like your ears. By doing this the ears become very sensitive and you pick up external sounds. Now this practice isn't, of course, to get you distracted by those sounds but rather to make mind more clear, make it extend outward so the level of attention to everything that is going on is greater.

Because this fault is one of losing attention and getting drowsy, you increase the attention by focusing on the sense powers and opening up more. Here the mind is likened to an eagle who is going fishing, scanning the waters and paying very close attention to what is going on out there in the water. At the very first sign of a fish coming near the surface, the eagle is ready to dive down and catch it. Meditation requires just such a state of mind, very alert and very aware of what is going on.

10   QUESTIONS AND ANSWERS II

What is the antidote to scattering of mind?

This was not discussed, but that's what we actually do in the "*HUNG*" exercises. The antidote to sinking is to open the eyes more, open the senses and increase the attention. Then we apply an antidote to scattering, the tendency of mind to get out of control, by relaxing the body from the inside. The posture is not relaxed, but the attention is gathered to the center and relaxed. That brings mind back under control.

What do I do about distractions?

There are two types of distractions: external sounds and internal sensations, such as warmth or whatever you are feeling inside. These function as distractions if you allow mind to focus on them. The best thing to do is not pay attention to them. Return to the object of concentration, whatever that is, and just ignore the external sounds or internal sensations. Simply ignore them and return mind to its proper object of focus.

If the nature of mind can be realized with shamatha and vipashyana meditation, why do we need Vajrayana practices, like visualization, saying prayers, and so forth?

Shamatha and vipashyana hold a very important place in practice. In the context of the development of an overall practice, they are what make it useful, what make it able to achieve its goal. Without the context of practice, the development of the different types of realization is not so useful. So, if the prayers, visualizations—things which appear to have a ritual aspect to them—are practiced correctly and are understood properly, they are absolutely necessary. They are what build up merit and get rid of defilements, and that is precisely what allows shamatha and vipashyana to actually be developed. Without building up merit and getting rid of defilements, these will not take place.

Lord Jigten Sumgön specified that one's practice has to be inclusive, sort of a holistic approach that takes into account the practitioner's entire situation and the world or the environment. It cannot separate out certain things to emphasize and neglect others. Rather, it is a comprehensive path of development which allows the disciple to develop completely and proceed along the stages of development. Otherwise, if one just tries to practice the most advanced method without doing anything to build up to it, then there is no possibility of success.

Now, when we speak of shamatha and vipashyana, these two elements are present at every stage of practice. Shamatha is anything which focuses mind and eliminates all the extraneous mental activities. Vipashyana is anything that develops insight. These exist at all times with any religious practice, when done properly.

For instance, when focusing on a visualization in the generation stage of any Tantra, one is necessarily practicing shamatha, mental quiescence, without which there is no way to hold the object of visualization. So, the object of visualization in the generation stage functions in the same way as the simple object in the most basic stages of our practice of mental quiescence. So you should understand that the same is true with vipashyana. As we go through these practices, if we are really paying attention to what we are doing, to what the verses that we recite are saying, they are helping us to develop insight into the nature of reality.

What is the difference between focusing on internal sensation and relaxing, as an antidote to scattering?

The antidote meditation is sort of a releasing, a letting go, a relaxing. It is not a focusing. You are not focusing one-pointedly on some sensation; rather, it's just a sort of letting go. You just relax rather than taking up that sensation as an object of meditation.

Some Western scientists believe that the mind consists only of chemical reactions and electrical impulses that reside in the brain and can be measured with very elaborate equipment. Can that view be reconciled with the Buddhist view of mind?

The Buddhist view of mind has three characteristics:

(1) the essential substance of mind, which is said to be emptiness;
(2) the nature of mind, which is said to be clarity; and
(3) the aspect or quality of mind, which is said to be unobstructed, in the sense that it does not arise, abide, or cease.

Of these distinguishing traits of mind, the first one seems to go along with what you're saying about Western science. The reason is, when we say emptiness, that means that something does not exist by way of its own nature. Rather, it arises only in dependence upon causes and conditions. That seems to be the one characteristic from these three that is held in common. From what you say of the Western view, mind arises only when you have all the causes and conditions of the gray matter and the chemical and electrical functions. If any of these were absent, then you wouldn't have mind. So that much is in common—that mind, like all phenomena, arises not by way of its own nature, but through the arising of proper causes and conditions.

How about Western atomic theories of matter and energy—what do the Buddhists think of them?

This is an interesting subject. To do it justice would take a lot of time, especially because you have in Western philosophy a number of very different viewpoints on this question of subject and object. Now in Buddhism, philosophy is divided into four different schools of philosophical views and tenets. The first two are called Vaibhashika and Sautrantika. Both of them accept an external world composed of truly existent objects, which are formed out of substances like atomic particles. They accept the existence of partless particles. The smallest units of matter build up a truly existent external world. Both these schools are associated most closely with Hinayana Buddhism.

Then you have the third school, the Vijñanavada. In the Vijñanavada you do not have an external world whose entity is different than mind itself. (Here, when we say "external," it refers to the object or to the objective world; "internal" means mind or the subject.) They do not say that external objects do not exist, but rather that the essential substance of the external world is not different from that of mind itself.

In the fourth, the Madhyamika school, there is a refutation of the very idea of existence, of subject and object, so to say that either subject or object exists would be a mistake. To say that they do not exist is also a mistake. That is why it is called the Middle Way, or Madhyamika. It refutes both of the extremes—existence and non-existence—being ultimately different from each other. Of course, conventionally they are different. While appearing to be different, ultimately they are not. That is why it is said that they have one taste. At their very essence, they are the same.

How does meditation work? Why does it lead to Buddhahood?

Again, this is a deep question, but we will try to approach an answer to it. The Buddhist understanding of the function of mind is that it's very complex and has many layers. Among

these, there are so-called latencies, or propensities, of mind.
This seems to roughly correspond with the conception of the
subconscious, that mind has the ability to hold the latencies,
or propensities, which are based upon former experiences,
especially former experiences which were very influential.
These are held in mind as a potential and then arise at a later
point. So, what we are doing in the process of meditation is
dealing with the subconscious by allowing those propensities to arise and disappear. In other words, they arise in meditation as the kalpana and, if one is able to release them, they
disappear.

By meditating, using all these processes for generating oneself as a deity and focusing the mind one-pointedly on an
object, one is also establishing propensities for the future. All
this is sort of rebuilding the subconscious along a new pat-
tern so that, in the future, the latencies we are planting now
will eventually manifest in the form of Buddhahood. We will
become Buddhas on the basis of what we do now in our meditation practice.

If there is no inherent existence, what use is compassion?

When we speak of a lack of inherent existence, we must
understand it as a universal characteristic of all phenomena.
If you focus on just that and realize the non-inherent existence of all phenomena but do not have any other aspect to
your practice, this will block your progress. You come up
against a wall, and can't progress farther. If you really perfect this, if you really see the ultimate nature of things in their
lack of inherent existence, then you are no longer bound to
anything in samsara, and you attain nirvana. But that functions as a sort of stopping point, a blank wall. You can't go
any farther; you can't achieve the benefits of living beings.
You can't even achieve your own ultimate benefit. You're
stuck! You have to go back and develop compassion in order
to achieve Buddhahood because compassion cuts the other
extreme view, clinging to the concept of non-inherent existence, or nihilism. Wisdom and compassion are developed

separately and joined together in the practice so as to obtain Buddhahood. It happens only through joining these together. So it's important not to emphasize the absence of inherent existence too much. One has to always develop compassion and join those two together. Then there is no problem in attaining Buddhahood.

Why was the syllable HUNG selected for the meditation exercise? How is it special or different from other syllables?

The syllable *HUNG* is rich with symbolism and can be interpreted in many ways. For instance, five distinct components make up the syllable, and these symbolize the five wisdoms. There are many other ways in which it could be interpreted as well. However, the usage of the syllable *HUNG* in the meditations described above does not depend upon any symbolic meaning. In general, you could say it's used because it has very important symbolic meaning included in other practices and is, therefore, a good thing to use. But it has no specific import in this meditation. You don't have to know any of its meanings to perform the meditation. Its usage in this meditation is more to mediate between the subject and the object—you dissolve the external world into *HUNG* syllables of various sizes and then bring these in and dissolve the internal world into it also. Working with that method is very useful, but you could use some other image also.

Where in mind is karma?

Simply put, what holds the propensities that carry the karma, what holds the kleshas and all these things, is a subtle consciousness which goes on from one moment to the next. You could think of it as a continuum from one moment to the next, that goes on from one life to another.

11 THE ATTAINMENT OF NON-ATTAINMENT

Once, Tilopa advised his disciple to go off to an isolated retreat and avoid any meditation. Now, this may seem a little
unusual for a meditation retreat. He explains, however, that
when you go to meditate, you normally take up something
to meditate on, some *thing*. That thing, and therefore that
meditation, is necessarily artificial. The practice of Mahamudra is not like that at all. It is not taking up a thing called
Mahamudra and meditating on it. Ultimately, Mahamudra
practice is meditation directly on reality itself.

Reality itself is not something devised or made up. What
you have to do here is accustom yourself to that, practice
that. You are not taking up a meditation, but rather are practicing something. Like any activity, when you practice and
become accustomed to it, it becomes easier and easier. So,
acquaint yourself with this lack of anything whatsoever to
be taken up as a discrete object. Focus on reality itself and
become accustomed to that. Tilopa's advice, then, is that if
you attain *something* by this Mahamudra practice, then you
have not attained Mahamudra. Attaining Mahamudra is attaining non-attainment. If you are not getting anything, then
you're getting Mahamudra. If you get some *thing*, then necessarily it is not Mahamudra.

What is the meaning of this? If, when we strive for Buddhahood, we think that Buddhahood is something that we are going to get, we will be making a great mistake. We would be like hunters going after an animal. Buddhahood would be reduced to just another worldly activity in which we engage to get some pleasure for ourselves. Mahamudra is not like that, it is not some thing to be obtained. It is attaining the state of non-attainment. Understanding that, we do not focus on obtaining something but on transcending. We have to get beyond that search for something to grasp onto.

Now the nature of reality is beyond the illusion of the phenomenal world, the world as it appears. What appears is illusory; reality is something else. So, when engaging in this meditation on Mahamudra, one seeks to realize Mahamudra. As long as it is something that is an object of mind, something that is conceived by mind, then is it necessarily something other than Mahamudra. Mahamudra is not a conception, not something which is of the nature of appearances or of the nature of objects of the conventional mind.

Therefore, whatever we look for, whatever we try to hold on to in terms of objects of mind, is not going to be Mahamudra. It is something other than that. It is not of the nature of the phenomenal world in any sense. As long as we conceive of it as something, we are making a mistake and will not attain the realization of Mahamudra in that way. Tilopa's advice is that if the disciple wishes to see Mahamudra, the disciple must go beyond conventional mind and abandon worldly involvement, because the conventional mind and worldly activities are what obscure the realization of Mahamudra and can never lead to it.

Search, then, for mind itself. Search for the perceiver or the meditator, the essential nature of the one who is seeking the realization. Turn your search inward and seek mind itself. Abandon all the coverings of mind which are like clothing—all the things which are associated with it and which one thinks of in terms of what mind is. All of these are like clothing, and the search is for the naked mind, the unclothed mind, mind in its very essential essence. All of the conventional attributes of mind are just concepts, things we must transcend in order to penetrate to the very core of the essential mind itself. To see the nature of reality, to realize Mahamudra, it is necessary to abandon involvement in the world.

In practice, this actually means to get rid of inner involvements. Inner involvements are the kleshas, the unwholesome negative mental activities of desire, aversion, delusion, and so forth. These are what must be abandoned, or dispelled. The technique for dispelling these is the practice of shamatha. The example given here is a pool of water. If you want to see the depths of the water, one must clear out the mud, the defilements, in the water that makes it impossible for you to see the bottom. So the kleshas—greed, hatred, delusion, and so forth—are like the mud that fills the pond. Until all that mud settles out, you cannot see the bottom. It is the practice of mental quiescence that allows all of these kleshas to cease.

Then with vipashyana, you can see through the clear water to the essential nature of reality. And so, the realization of Mahamudra is not the creation of something which was not there, nor is it the removal of something. In other words, to realize Mahamudra you do not get rid of or abandon appearances; they are not what is obstructing the view. Appearances can be allowed to stand just as they are. Nor is there anything to be achieved or produced. There is nothing to be obtained from reality to realize Mahamudra. Rather, through the practice of mental quiescence, allow the disturbing tendencies to subside and then reality will appear by itself.

The realization of ultimate reality can be approached in various ways by developing insight through establishing the correct philosophical view. With regard to the various inner and outer phenomena, one can gradually learn the right and the wrong in terms of the view and develop the realization of one thing after another. In this way, a realization can gradually build up. However, the most effective way is to get at the very root of delusion and cut it off. Once this is cut off, the trunk, the leaves, the stems, and the branches of the tree of illusion will wither and die. So rather than remove them one at a time, it's best to go right to the root of delusion.

The way this is done in practice is to look at the essential nature of mind. Once that has been realized in its true nature, the root of delusion is destroyed and all the delusions with regard to all other appearances of the world will cease. The realities of the inner and outer worlds will be realized together. Through this process of realizing ultimate reality by looking at the essential nature of mind itself, the root of all delusion is destroyed and one sees reality, the inner and outer, as it actually is.

In the process of doing this, one also removes all the defilements from beginningless time. In all of our past lifetimes—from countless ages ago—we have accumulated vast negative karma, incalculable non-virtuous activities and defilements. If we tried to apply antidotes to each of these and purify them one by one, it would be an interminable task. However, by cutting the root of delusion, we cut the root of all these defilements and remove them all at once. So the direct view, the direct realization of the ultimate truth of Mahamudra, in and of itself destroys all the defilements accumulated from beginningless time.

The practical instructions for engaging in the meditation leading to Mahamudra are given here from the very beginning of the path. The priority at the beginning is to gain a sense of control whereby mind does not go this way and that, becoming attached to worldly appearances which make it impossible to progress in Mahamudra practice. This is where the practices related to mental quiescence come into play. The techniques to achieve it are described here. The various meditation techniques, like concentrating on the breath, are explained. The point is not control so much as it is unifying the essence of mind with the breath as it comes in and goes out.

This process can be compared to learning to drive a car. In the beginning, you have to learn how to steer in a rough sense so that the car stays on the road. Later you can drive efficiently and go to your destination. So, these things—like the breathing and the focus of your gaze—are the necessary controls. Once you gain proficiency in this, mind will settle down, and you can continue more efficiently in this path of meditation. By controlling the eyes and breath, mind itself comes under control.

Having gained control through these techniques, mind is then used to focus on mind itself. When mind focuses on mind itself, the kalpana arise, and these must be cleared away. Before mind can perceive itself, you must abandon all conceptual ideas; these are not mind. This is said to be like trying to find the center of the sky. The sky in this sense means the vastness of empty space. If we look for something that we can call the center, we will not find anything. Or if we look for the end of space, we will also not find anything. The very nature of space is that it is endless, so finding the center or an edge is impossible.

Similarly, when we look at mind and try to find characteristics like that, we will not find them. These characteristics are conceptual, they are the dichotomies between center and edge, or size or shape or color. We must go beyond these dichotomies of thought in order to see mind in its essential nature. Viewing the essential nature of mind is compared to viewing the ocean or the sky. If you look at the ocean superficially, your view is obscured by the waves on the surface. If you look at the sky, you just see clouds and not the sky. The waves on the ocean and the clouds in the sky are like the kalpana. If we go beyond the waves, we see the depths of the ocean. If we go beyond the clouds, we see the extent of the sky. Likewise, we have to go beyond the kalpana to see the mind. They disappear just like the waves on the ocean and the clouds in the sky. They are not permanent or abiding in their nature. So, by seeing the true nature of mind, all of these kalpana simply dissolve and disappear.

Taking the example of the sky, we can see that even though things like clouds appear in the sky, when they disappear, they leave no trace. Colors appear in the sky—the whiteness of dawn and the darkness of midnight. The darkness does not leave a stain; when the sun rises in the morning, it's all gone. Likewise, the colors of the day; although they appear in the sky, they are gone at night without a trace. So the nature of the sky itself is undefiled, unmarked, unstained by that which appears within it. Its nature is that it is non-composed. It is not made up of parts. It is not something which we can define in terms of size, shape, color, or form.

So, like that, mind has various contents which appear in it but do not leave a residue. They just disappear. Mind is also not definable by way of size, shape, color, extent, or any characteristics like that. In its essential nature, mind is identical with the Tathagatagarbha, Buddha-nature. It is also the wisdom of self-knowledge. The wisdom of self-knowledge and Buddha-nature are by their most intrinsic, basic quality free of all attributions. By realizing their nature, all of these adventitious contents are dissolved.

The nature of the mind is also compared to space. In empty space, various things arise—various appearances, material objects, worlds, suns, moons. All of these things arise in space and stay there for a very long time, moving this way and that. All of the activities of the world take place in space. But then everything moves on and the space that was filled at one time is empty at another time. Once all of the things have moved on and are no longer present in a certain space, that space is completely empty and completely free of any residue of all that took place there.

Likewise, mind. Although it has been engaged for countless eons since beginningless time in all sorts of activities, accumulating all sorts of karma and defilements, its very nature is completely unstained by all these things. When one realizes the clear light of reality, then all those stains completely disappear, leaving no residue whatsoever in mind.

12 TILOPA'S PITH INSTRUCTIONS

Tilopa's pith instructions are the essential teachings that are said to be like the root and the trunk of the tree of Mahamudra practice. So they should be heeded very carefully and always kept in mind. The title of the text we are following is *The Mahamudra of the Ganges*, so called because Tilopa taught it on the banks of the Ganges River. This is called the root text, the basic text which Tilopa taught. It has been expanded upon in great commentaries, but this teaching is from the root text itself—in Sanskrit, the *Mahamudra Upadesha*. *Mahamudra* is, of course, *chak-gya chenpo*, and *Upadesha* means essential teachings, or precepts.*

After the title, the text begins with the homage, saying, "I bow down to the simultaneously arisen." What is the meaning of "simultaneously arisen"? It means that phenomena, especially the subjects that observe objects, are in the objects themselves; they are simultaneously arisen. In other words, there is no earlier or later, no first or second, no beginning or end to the essential nature itself. Since it has existed since beginningless time, we can't even speak of earlier or later;

---

* A full translation of Tilopa's original text can be found in *The Myth of Freedom, and the Way of Meditation* (Boston: Shambala Publications, 1976), pp. 157-163 , by Chögyam Trungpa.

we must speak of arising simultaneously. This refers to phenomena as objects and their attributes. Or you could say phenomena and their essential nature, or their reality. These are all simultaneously arisen.

The example can be given of sugar and its sweetness. They arise together in the same way as fire and its heat. These are objects with their attributes. You can't speak of one arising first and the other next, but rather they arise simultaneously from the beginning. As with sugar and fire, so all phenomena together with their reality, or their essential attributes, exist together from the beginning.

Dharma Lord Gampopa said, "That which is simultaneously arisen with mind is the dharmakaya. Just like sugar and sweetness, mind and dharmakaya arise together from the very beginning." He also said, "That which arises simultaneously with appearances is the radiance of the dharmakaya." So, all appearances—all that we see, including our kalpana, our false, dualistic conceptions—all of these things arise simultaneously with what is called the radiance of the dharmakaya or the light given off by the dharmakaya. This obeisance, then, is to mind and the Dharmakaya, which arise simultaneously with appearances, which are the light of the dharmakaya.

The text says here that Mahamudra is not something that can be simply pointed out or demonstrated. It is not that type of thing. The explanation of this is that any ordinary phenomenon can be pointed out, demonstrated, or indicated in some fashion, but we cannot do that with Mahamudra. Why? The answer is that Mahamudra is reality itself, in the ultimate sense. It is absolute reality. And because of that, anything that we point out or indicate falls short of that reality. It is artificial, it arises from some dichotomy. Mahamudra is not that sort of thing. Rather, it is non-dual; it is ultimate reality. It is reality itself; therefore there is no easy way to point it out.

So, the realization of Mahamudra requires some exertion, some application of effort and concentration because it is not a simple thing or some worldly object. Because of this, those who seek to realize it must practice. The text mentions that someone like Naropa had to undergo twelve great trials in order to receive the essential teachings and realize Mahamudra. Not only that, but he had to prepare himself over a significant period of time by purifying all of his obscurations and accumulating great merit. Then he approached the teaching, made many requests, underwent many great hardships, and gradually was able to acquire the teachings and realize Mahamudra.

Tilopa begins the text saying, "Kye ho!" He is looking at the nature of the phenomenal world and saying, "Alas!" This great illusion wherein living beings wander constantly—whoever is born into this world must pass away and die. Whatever is built in this world eventually falls apart. Whatever is accumulated by the beings of the world is eventually dispersed. Every gathering of people and association of people, in the end, is lost, and everyone goes his own way. There is nothing whatsoever in this world that is permanent, abiding, or stable. There is nothing to be relied upon. Everything is impermanent, just like a mirage or a dream. There is nothing to place confidence in or rely upon.

The nature of impermanence is not only seen in the grosser forms such as the death of every living being, the destruction of everything that is built up, and the dispersal of everything that is accumulated, but it is the pervasive nature of all phenomena in the world. Everything changes moment by moment, instant by instant. When we say a word, that word goes out and never returns again. It appears to be there, but when we try to hold onto it, it is already lost. All phenomena are of that nature, subtly changing from instant to instant. There is nothing that can abide, nothing in the world that has any stability or any ability to stay beyond an instant.

So all phenomena are said to be like a cloud in the sky that is constantly moving and changing, disappearing and reappearing, but never truly able to abide or hold its own nature. There is nothing in the world that can do that. So the world is said to be like a show with many different appearances and sounds, but with no stability or reality behind it. It's just a performance. Understanding impermanence in both its gross and subtle forms leads us to realize that the world is like a dream or an illusion.

When we dream, we see and hear many things; we feel many things. It seems very real, but when we wake up, it's all gone. If we look for the reality of the houses, the people, the events, they're all gone. Like a bird flying across the sky— once it has flown away, there is no remainder, there is no trace left, nothing to be grasped. So, because of their impermanence, all phenomena are like that. They appear, they seem to be real, but a moment later they are gone. There is nothing left of what was there before. If we look at our lives up to this moment, if we look into the past, what we did years ago or last year or yesterday, it's gone, it's completely like a dream. When we see the nature of the present, we realize that things do not exist the way they appear to exist. There is absolutely nothing in all of these appearances that is firm or abiding.

That is not just true for us, but for all other living beings, even in the divine realms of the great long-lived gods. Even they pass away. Even their realms are changing moment by moment. So there is nothing to be found that is permanent. That's why all that appears to us in the conventional world lacks any true reality; nothing exists as it appears to exist. It is all empty. The ultimate nature of all things, then, is emptiness, the lack of any inherent existence, whereby they cannot abide and exist from their own side, as they appear. The world exists in this ephemeral and transitory way.

When we get caught up in the world and believe it to be something real, we act in certain ways that inevitably lead to misery. Therefore, it is said, all activities of the world are without essence, without any real meaning, and miserable by their very nature because they are based on the delusion that the world actually exists as it appears. They are based upon ignorance of the fact that the world is illusory and there is nothing there to grasp. When we attempt to grasp at things, we engage in actions which inevitably lead to misery. When we are born into the world, we experience the misery of birth, of sickness, of old age, of death—these are inevitable.

Once we take birth into the world, once we become involved in this illusion, then these things will happen to us and there is no escape. We are born into the world through craving. So when we crave or desire something and do not achieve it, that is one kind of misery. Then there's the misery of getting the many things that we don't want; there's the misery of not being able to meet with loved ones; there's the misery of finding oneself meeting with people one dislikes or who make one unhappy. All of these things are simply part of the world. Once we are involved in the world with all these illusions, there is no escape from these miseries.

The commentary includes a story which Tilopa told Naropa to illustrate this teaching about the lack of any essence in the world and how activities lead to miseries even when things go relatively well: The story is of a hunter in Tibet. Hunting was the only way he could make a living. He set out to catch an animal and bring it home. He went for many days, crossing over high mountain passes, getting hungrier and thirstier, and was unable to even see any animal to kill and bring home. So he faced this great misery of seeking but being unable to find. This went on for a while until finally he saw an animal, a mountain deer, which he shot with his bow and arrow. Although he hit it, he just wounded it. So he followed the trail of blood, and it went on and on and on. Finally, after a great search, he found the animal dead but only after experiencing all this additional misery. Then he loaded the animal up on his back and started the long journey home across the mountains. The dead animal was very heavy, and he suffered greatly from carrying it back and having to guard it against predators and thieves. Finally, he arrived home with the deer, completely exhausted. The people of his village were so happy to see him with this animal and praised him, saying how great he was, and, by the way, could they have just a little bit of the meat? By the time his family divided it up, giving little pieces to this person and that person, there was virtually nothing left for the hunter himself.

So this is Tilopa's analogy for the activities of people in the world—"their miseries of searching for a livelihood or searching for what they desire and being unable to find it; even when they find it, being unable to grasp it, once they grasp it; having nothing but misery in trying to hold on to it and not lose it. In the end when the time comes to enjoy it, there is very little, if anything, left to enjoy." The advice which Tilopa gave to Naropa was to always understand that this is the nature of the world and worldly activities and, through this understanding, to disengage from the world and from its activities.

There is no way to practice and obtain liberation and Buddhahood while engaging in worldly activities, while caught up in the illusion of the world, attached to it and unable to let go. That condition is contrary to the requirements of practice. And so Tilopa advises his disciple to retreat to a place that is isolated from the busyness and involvement and entanglements of the world. There, he should detach himself and disengage from society and the world. Only then can one have a real opportunity to practice effectively.

To return to the initial statement about Mahamudra—Tilopa said that Mahamudra is not simple, not something that can be pointed out. It's not this thing or that thing or some other thing. It is reality itself. This is again illustrated with the example of empty space. Empty space is non-composite; it's not made up of anything; it doesn't have parts. And so, when we speak of empty space, we can use various examples but can't really point to something and make someone understand empty space in its entirety. That is not the nature of space. Likewise, the clear light of mind can be compared to the light of the sun, but that also is not an accurate comparison and it is not very enlightening. The clear light of mind or of reality itself—this is what must be experienced directly, not understood through analogies or similes. Ultimately, it cannot be understood through these things, but must be directly perceived. If we think about the nature of empty space and how we might point to it or describe it, we can see how imprecise this method is. We can only describe individual objects. Even then, our descriptions are always going to be mere indicators and not the objects themselves. When we really try to define or point out something as subtle and difficult to grasp as empty space, we can only do it in a rough way. So there has to be a leap of cognition in which we leave the conceptual level to experience the actual thing.

Now, attempting to describe empty space is very difficult. All we have is a conception and, when we try to grasp what it actually is, this conception does not take us very far. Yet still we feel that we know what it is. The nature of mind itself is much more subtle than that. We cannot even roughly grasp it conceptually. However, by clearing away these attempts at conceptually grasping mind, we can proceed to see it directly. From the very outset of approaching a realization of the nature of mind, we have to abandon conceptual attempts. By understanding their futility, we abandon any idea of building it up or creating something in our minds which accurately describes or reflects the nature of mind. We must first abandon these attempts as being completely futile. Therefore, in the meditation, we have to cultivate this sense of letting go of all attempts to construct a viable hypothesis of what the nature of mind is. These things just tie mind in knots and do not reveal its nature. The example is given here of tying a knot in a snake. If you attempt to untie it, it is very difficult; but if you just let the snake go, it will unravel itself.

Describing mind as empty space is describing reality itself. Reality itself is like empty space. In its very nature, it cannot be grasped conceptually; nothing can be grasped conceptually. It is not that we are trying to find this thing called mind and extract it from of the rest of reality. In fact, all reality, ultimate reality, essential reality, is beyond grasping and is like empty space itself. Ultimately, when we practice approaching the realization of Mahamudra, there has to be an abandonment of all types of mental, physical, and verbal activity. The very nature of all of these is dichotomizing and, accordingly, they obstruct the realization of the nature of reality.

Now, when Dharma Lord Gampopa first went to Jetsun Milarepa to receive teachings, he was already very accomplished in the study of the Dharma. He had been a disciple in the Kadampa lineage for a long time. He had been engaged in very high-level practices involving various meditations and visualizations, verbal activities like reciting mantras, physical activities like making tormas—all sorts of religious practices. Milarepa said this was very good and worthwhile, and a great result had ripened and developed in him. However, to realize the truth, to manifest the realization of Mahamudra, in the end all of these things have to be abandoned. All involvements of body, speech, and mind have to be released so that the nature of reality can be realized. The nature of reality does not involve creating or achieving something or building something up. Rather, it is letting go of all that is false, of all that is limited, of all that involves the nature of the world— everything that involves any type of dichotomy or conceptual thought.

The physical body is compared to a reed that grows in the water. The reed appears to be substantial but is actually completely hollow. Likewise, the body appears to be substantial, something important, but really it has no essence. Mind itself is like the empty sky, without attributes of center or edge or color or shape. To realize the nature of mind, one has to ultimately let go, just completely let go of all striving, of all creative mental activity. Just abandon all of these things which involve dichotomies. Mind is not subject to specifications like "it is this or it is that or it is the other thing." As long as we try to specify what mind is, we will always be lost and will never find its essential nature.

So what has to be done to stop specifying what mind is? Stop assuming what it is and thinking of it in one way or another. Then go on to accustom mind completely to that state

of non-specification, non-construction, non-dichotomizing.
Once mind becomes completely accustomed, completely
comfortable in that state of non-specification, then one can
realize Mahamudra.

Mind has nothing in its essential nature that can be identified. There is nothing there to be specified, identified, or pointed
out because its nature is clarity. There is nothing within it, there
is no part of it or quality that can be separated out and identified. So, getting beyond that, one arrives at the stage of finding the path to Buddhahood through this non-specification,
this non-identification of the nature of reality, and by becoming accustomed to this state which is free of all kalpanas.

The path itself becomes a non-path, a path which is ultimately not specifiable. Becoming accustomed to that path,
one achieves the path of Buddhahood. The attainment of the
state of perfect Buddhahood arises from the practice of ac-
customing oneself to the state of non-identifiability, non-
conceptualization, the state of mind which does not create or
produce any conceptions, does not create anything artificial,
but rather lets go of all this creative mental activity. This allows ultimate reality itself to manifest and be realized without projecting anything upon it, or separating anything out
of it, just allowing it to shine forth. This requires exertion.
This requires focusing mind on this state, which is beyond
all conceptualizations.

Then we have the three necessary aspects of view, meditation, and activity:

(1) The view of Mahamudra is that which is completely
    beyond the dualism of subject and object. It is the aban-
    donment, or renunciation, of the dualism of subject and
    object.

(2) The highest meditation is that which is free of all wa-
    vering or distraction. Mind is set in such a way that it
    is completely free of any type of movement.

(3) The highest activity is that which abandons all discrimi-
    nation—all choosing the better thing, rejecting the worse

thing, making discriminations between this and that. The highest activity is beyond that sort of discrimination.

The highest result, which is the attainment of Maha-mudra, arises only when one transcends all hopes and fears. As long as one is caught up in hoping for something, for some very good state (Buddhahood or something else), as long as one cherishes a hope for that and also fears falling into a lower state, one is caught up in a condition which is beneath the highest realization. One has to go beyond that, abandon hopes and fears. In that state free of hopes and fears, Mahamudra is obtained.

The text now repeats itself, again going over what the very highest view is and what the meditation activities are and so forth. It goes into a little more detail here, specifying, for instance, the very highest view. Before, it said that this is the view which is beyond the dichotomy of subject and object. This state of transcending the view of subject and object is that state which is free of extremes. The extremes have to do with that which is internal or external. All of these are relative views, the views that some thing exists in some way relative to something else. From the perspective of something else, we can speak of subject and object. But ultimate reality is beyond all such dichotomies and such limitations of perspective because it is all-inclusive.

Now again, the meaning of the state of the highest meditation is briefly explained. The highest meditation is one in which mind does not waver at all. The wavering here is not just wavering from the object of meditation, but it is wavering to any type of limited view that is only relatively true. Hold one-pointedly to the absolute which is without any specifications or determinations. The highest result, or goal, is the realization of the ultimate nature of mind itself. Therefore, any goal that entails an achievement or an attainment or an obtaining of something is always short of the ultimate goal. That is because as long as one's self is attaining something or realizing something, then there is still the self and the other, still some sort of dichotomy. Yet the very ultimate goal is the self in its very essence. It is not the self attaining something other than the essential self. Therefore, that is the highest goal, which is free of any dichotomy whatsoever.

The practice that we engage in to reach this ultimate result, of course, entails exertion on the path of mental quiescence. This is the substance of our practice from now until we obtain the ultimate goal of perfect enlightenment. This journey of developing the state of mental quiescence is compared to a great river like the Ganges in India. When we start to practice shamatha, it is like the Ganges in its uppermost headwaters in the region of Mt. Kailash. It's just a tiny little stream that at the beginning has stops and starts with a lot of rocks and obstacles in its way; it is very tentative. At this point, it is very vulnerable. As it goes downstream it is very turbulent, going over great rocks and rapids. Gradually it gets stronger and wider. It comes down to the plain where it's a tremendously large and deep river that flows swiftly. Accomplishing mental quiescence is like this—the stream of meditation is very powerful and cannot be blocked or disturbed. It just flows very strongly. Then finally it meets the great ocean, and at this point it is boundless and unfathomable and stays completely still. That is the simile used to illustrate the nature of this practice of mental quiescence, which leads to the goal of Mahamudra.

We should understand that none of the preliminary practices are able to reveal the clear light of Mahamudra in and of themselves. All of these practices—meditation, the cultivation of virtue, the practices of discipline and ethics, the practices of Tantra—all these things in themselves contribute along the way to the stream of the river, develop it and lead it to its goal. But none of them alone can be expected to reveal the clear light of Mahamudra. It is through the practice of meditation that one gradually becomes freer and freer of all attachment and clinging, first of the gross aspects of existence of the world and then of the subtler and subtler, until one becomes completely free of all clinging to physical, verbal, and mental events or objects. One becomes free of all dichotomies and, therefore, comes to realize the meaning of all three baskets of the Buddha's teaching. This is the ultimate realization of the clear light of Mahamudra.

Through realizing, by merely seeing the clear light of Mahamudra, the doors to the prison of samsara swing open. One is released from the bondage of cyclic existence. Then, by practicing and stabilizing mind on that clear light of Mahamudra, all of the gross and subtle defilements of body, speech, and mind from beginningless time are completely burned away and eliminated, and the highest state of perfect enlightenment is attained.

First, one becomes fearful of falling into the tremendous miseries of the lower forms of life in cyclic existence, all of the lower migrations. Approaching the realization of Mahamudra and becoming free of this fear, one is filled with compassion for all of those living beings who helplessly wander in samsara, falling again and again into the inconceivable miseries of the lower realms. Powered by that great compassion, one practices these essential precepts of the Lord Buddha's teaching and attains full insight into ultimate reality, which occurs when mind becomes stabilized in Mahamudra. One thereby attains the state of Buddhahood, which alleviates all of these miseries.

Tilopa makes a dedication at the end of this text for the welfare of all beings:

> By the virtue of full engagement in this practice, may all
>   obstacles to realization of Mahamudra dissolve away.
> May the clear light of Mahamudra dawn in the minds
>   of disciples.
> May all living beings then come to abide in the hearts
>   of those disciples who realize Mahamudra.

13   DHARMA LORD GAMPOPA'S ADVICE

We will now look at Lord Gampopa's advice on how to deal with the various problems that arise in the practice of Mahamudra meditation. First, in order to avoid errors, one must have a fully qualified lama—that is, a teacher who has actually experienced the realization of Mahamudra. The teacher should not be one in name only, but should be someone who has accomplished this path, has knowledge and experience, and who is thereby able to lead others. The student should be one who maintains awareness of the truth of impermanence and death and, motivated by that, exerts him- or herself in this practice. He should be able to recognize the fully qualified teacher as being a manifestation of the Buddha himself in the world. So, for the practice to succeed or for the actual practice to even begin, there must be the coming together of a qualified teacher and a qualified student.

When looking for a fully qualified teacher, we don't need to think in terms of the great enlightened beings of the past such as Dharma Lord Gampopa other, these ultimately accomplished and realized beings. Rather, it is sufficient to have a teacher who has experience in and realization of

Mahamudra, though that teacher may be far short of the supreme attainment of the great teachers. Still, if the teacher has a genuine practice of Mahamudra or a true realization of Mahamudra, then that is sufficient to qualify that teacher to transmit the instruction and guide the practice of the disciple.

The disciple, in turn, must be qualified not only by the understanding of impermanence and death, but, beyond that, by having a true appreciation of cause and effect. That is to say, he or she must not be one who is negligent of the principle of moral causation, but keeps that in mind. Also, the disciple should be one who has purified his or her defilements and amassed some merit in the lifetimes leading up to meeting the qualified teacher.

Once this coming together of student and teacher occurs, then the path must be traversed correctly. That is, one must go straight along the path and not fall off to one side or the other. Falling off the path, straying from the correct path of meditation leading to the Mahamudra, is described here principally in four ways:

(1) The first error is to mistake a facsimile or a representation of reality for actual reality. "Reality" refers to reality in its ultimate sense; it means Mahamudra, or emptiness. Here, one falls from the path by relying on a mere intellectual understanding of reality, no matter how good the understanding is, instead of actually experiencing it.

This can be compared to someone who wishes to go to Bodhgaya and asks someone what it is like. The other person has been there and can describe it in detail—all about the road leading up to Bodhgaya, where it turns and where there is a line of trees and where there are temples and where the great stupa is. Even if the second person describes it with great care and detail, the one who has not been there but wishes to go can, at best, only create a mental picture of what it is like. That mental picture will be something of his own devising and will never be the actual thing. If, rather than going there and seeing for himself, he is content with that facsimile, that made-up image in his own mind, then he will fall from the path. So, the person who wants to really see Bodhgaya must go there personally; he cannot be satisfied with the accounts of others.

Likewise, the person who wishes to realize Mahamudra, and with it gain freedom from all limitations and defilements and the attainment of all good qualities, must actually traverse the path and experience it herself with her own mind and not rely on the accounts of others. If one just learns to say that the ultimate nature is without arising, without abiding, and without ceasing and goes no further, one will have nothing much to show for one's effort. However, if one meditates properly, following the advice and precepts of a qualified teacher, one will attain direct insight and then be able to look back on those verses and understand their truth directly. Lord Jigten Sumgön said that it is absolutely indispensable for progress on this path and the attainment of its goal to rely properly upon a qualified spiritual teacher in the beginning, in the middle, and at the end.

(2) The second way of falling from the path is to believe that the attainment of full realization of Mahamudra, the ultimate attainment of perfect Buddhahood, means to leave everything behind and change into something else, to stop being a living person and become a Buddha, as if that were something entirely different. This is a great error which causes one to fall from the path by trying to transform oneself into something that one is not.

The example here is of a child who is born the son of a king. That child might think that when he finally grows up and ascends the throne, he will be something entirely different, and that of course is an error. Just as the prince is a human being, so the king is a human being. There is no sudden transformation into something that one is not. Likewise, the mind of an ordinary human being is not disposed of or left behind. Upon attaining Buddhahood, one does not adopt a new mind or become something totally other than what one was. By thinking this way, one loses sight of the path and falls off.

The verse says that becoming a Buddha is to become completely what one already is. To fully manifest the nature of mind is to become fully enlightened; it is not a case of gaining something that does not exist now. Even the highest state of perfect Buddhahood is not other than the nature of one's mind as it presently is.

(3) The next error which causes one to stray from this path of meditation is to believe that the conceptual mental processes, the kalpana, are something which have to be completely rejected and the pure mind something to be sought separately from those kalpana. This is a subtle error which misunderstands the relationship between the conceptual and dualistic thoughts of mind and mind itself. One thinks that they are something wholly other than mind and, so, tries to grasp a mind that is totally separate or divorced from them, when in fact they are of the same nature as mind.

The example given here is of a plant or tree with great medicinal properties. The medicinal properties of the tree pervade its entirety from its root through its trunk to its branches and leaves. Mistakenly thinking that the medicinal properties are found only in one part, one could inadvertently discard some of the best parts of the tree. So the conceptual processes of mind are not other than mind. Their nature is of mind itself. By trying to exclude them, to cut them off without recognizing their nature and their source, one will never be able to realize mind as it actually is.

(4) Just as mind and its contents should not be separated or thought of as being of different natures, so appearances and emptiness should not be distinguished in that way. This is the fourth way people fall from the correct path: by seeking an emptiness that is an ultimate reality apart from appearances. Thinking that appearances exist in their own right and that emptiness is something to be found elsewhere, they go in search of this emptiness excluding all appearances. This

is completely wrong. Appearances themselves are emptiness, emptiness is not apart from them. It says in the *Prajnaparamita*, "Form is emptiness and emptiness itself is form; form is no other than emptiness nor is emptiness other than form." The same is true with all the constituents of existence other than form, such as sensations, concepts, compositional factors in consciousness, or mind itself. All of these things are emptiness. Emptiness appears as these things and to seek emptiness elsewhere is to make a great mistake and fall off the correct path.

While practicing Mahamudra correctly and proceeding along the path, one encounters different levels of realization. It is very important not to become attached to any of those levels and mistake them as being the ultimate level of realization. If one does that, then one will certainly get stuck in one of the form or formless realms. So as one's meditation improves, as one gets higher and higher, one comes to stages which are like vast emptiness where one's perception, whether one's eyes are open or closed, is only of vast emptiness and peace. An experience like that could be mistaken for the realization of Mahamudra. If this occurs, and one thinks it is the ultimate goal and finds satisfaction, this causes rebirth in the form realm.

Likewise, as obstacles are cleared away in Mahamudra meditation, one attains a state of great peace and happiness, characterized by a very high and pure level of bliss. One can become attached to experiencing that bliss. If one becomes attached to it and holds onto that attachment, then at the time of death, one will be reborn in one of the heavens of the desire realm.

If one practices the meditation on Mahamudra and goes beyond these stages of great bliss, one will come to a stage of emptiness. If one does not become attached to that, one will go on to a state of absolute purity, where there is nothing whatsoever. One has then gone beyond all appearances, all things which could be called existent or non-existent. This is said to be the state of complete nothingness. This state seems so pure and absolutely free, one can become attached to it.

If one dies clinging to that state, one will be reborn in one of the levels of the formless realm. Because of this, then, it is vitally important as one proceeds in the practice not to become attached to anything, not to any appearance, feeling, sensation, or perception.

Now, avoiding these four ways in which one falls from the path and the three ways in which one gets caught being reborn into the heavenly realms, if one proceeds on the path of Mahamudra without error, then there are three different results depending upon the quality of one's exertion and practice:

(1) The very highest quality results in one's attaining in that very life, on that very seat of meditation, the state of perfect, peerless enlightenment equal to that of the Buddhas of the past, present, and future, beyond which there is nothing greater nor any enlightenment more complete. This highest state of perfect enlightenment is said to be like the sun rising up in the empty sky, free of all clouds, crystal clear. The sun rises and shines with all of its brilliance—this is the highest level of attainment in this path of Mahamudra.

(2) The middle level of attainment is compared to the sun arising in a sky that has clouds in it. Sometimes the brilliance of the sun will be seen in all its glory, then a moment later it will be obscured or there will be some shading of the sun. Then later it will come out again only to be obscured once again. This is the middle level, where one has a realization of ultimate reality but it does not last. There is some hesitation and doubt, and one loses the realization. Practicing some more, it comes back for awhile only to be lost again. When one is at this level in the practice, it is of great importance to rely on the qualified spiritual teacher to lead one beyond these final obstacles.

(3) The third, or lowest, type of realization attained through the proper practice of the path of Mahamudra is said to be like the sun shining in a deep canyon. One is down in a deep

canyon where it is dark and suddenly the sun shines, but then it's gone and doesn't come back. One gets a glimpse of it but cannot see it again. If this is the case, one has to rely on the spiritual teacher. The fault here is really in the relationship between meditation and realization. There was a realization at this point, but the meditation was not sufficient. Meditation really means becoming accustomed to or becoming practiced in something. So, one has to become accustomed to that realization so that it is not just a brief flash of insight. Rather, that flash is stabilized and internalized so that it remains and becomes unshakable. It does not disappear in clouds of doubt nor is it obscured by walls of delusion. This requires great exertion in the meditation to extend the realization and make it firm.

These three levels are also distinguished by the practitioners: those with the best practice, the sharpest faculties, and greatest diligence; those with the middle level of faculties and diligence; and those with the lower level. These three types of practitioners will gain these three types of results. It is not enough to have mere intellectual understanding; personal experience of these practices is essential. With the support of shamatha and other means of investigation, we must practice the nature of mind. Then as we progress, different experiences will arise. This yogic, or experiential, path is distinguished by way of four levels of practice:

(1) The first level of practice is called the "one-pointed yoga." Through one-pointed yoga, one arrives at a certain insight into the nature of mind, you could say the clear light of mind. However, because the focus is so narrow, a question arises subsequently in one's mind. That question is whether this was an experience or a conceptual realization. In other words, did one actually see it, or did one think one saw it? Did one convince oneself that this was true? So, whether it was conceptual or a directly perceived realization, is in doubt at this point.

(2) The second level of realization is called the "yoga which is free from projection." This means that one has arrived at the stage of perceiving one's own mind in terms of its lack of production, abiding, and cessation. One realizes that the nature of mind is free of these three extremes.

(3) The third level is called the "yoga of one taste." This means that one is able to perceive all phenomena, internal and external, subject and object, as being of one taste, just like sugar is of one taste. No matter what different types of objects sugar is formed into, they all taste sweet. They all have that same taste because they are all of the same essential nature. Likewise, subject and object, inner and outer, all phenomena—whether mind itself or mind's objects—are of one taste.

(4) The final stage of yogic meditation is called "that which is free of meditation and non-meditation." At this level of meditation, there is no longer any way to distinguish between the meditative session and the subsequent state of consciousness. In other words, there is no difference between the state of realization when one is engaged in meditation and the state of consciousness when one leaves the state of meditation. At this point the practice has become complete. There is nothing more to learn. This is the state of perfect enlightenment, or Buddhahood.

To use a worldly example, you could say that this path of meditation is like learning to drive a car. In the beginning it takes a lot of effort, there is a lot of doubt and hesitation. You constantly need to think of all the different things to do, and trying to do them all at the same time requires great effort and a lot of concentration. There are various dangers and many mistakes one can make. Gradually, one becomes more and more accustomed to it, and so it requires less effort and is more natural. Finally, in the end when one gains complete mastery over the process of driving a car, one gets into the car and arrives at one's destination almost without thinking about driving. One's mind is thinking about other things because driving a car has become completely natural.

Meditation is like that. When one attains this final level of meditation, it's really like not meditating at all, therefore it is called non-meditation. Even though it is a profound state of meditation, there is no entering the meditative state or leaving it. One's mind constantly abides in that perfect and complete knowledge.

These four levels can be correlated with the former three categories of the greater, middle, and lesser practitioners. Each of them applies to these four stages of practice. We can distinguish one's progress on this path of Mahamudra with many variations and levels. The stages of this path were outlined by Phagmo Drupa in accordance with the teachings of Dharma Lord Gampopa. He combined Gampopa's teachings on these four levels of yogic attainment with the three levels of practitioners, making twelve different levels of practice.

(1) The first level of yogic attainment was called the "one-pointed yoga," where mind becomes stabilized on its object. That is, it can hold an object one-pointedly without distraction, without losing it for a certain amount of time. So, one-pointed meditative concentration can exist at various levels; it can be held more or less firmly for different lengths of time. If we look at this from the point of view of the practitioners:

The lesser practitioner is able to hold clear concentration at times and loses it sometimes.

The middle-level practitioner is able to maintain stable concentration so long as effort is being exerted. In other words, as long as that individual wishes to hold an object one-pointedly in mind, that object will remain in focus without distraction. Even between sessions when the individual practitioner is not trying to do it, sometimes that object will arise spontaneously and can be held one-pointedly. But it will always appear one-pointedly when the practitioner so desires.

Low Level Practitioner

One-pointed Yoga	Sporadic concentration
Yoga Free from Projection	Limited view of reality
Yoga of One Taste	Unity of all phenomena
Yoga Free of Meditation and Non-meditation	Unbroken flow of realization

Middle Level Practitioner

One-pointed Yoga	Consistent concentration with effort
Yoga Free from Projection	Penetration to the root of reality
Yoga of One Taste	Fullness of non-duality
Yoga Free of Meditation and Non-meditation	Effortless manifestation of the three bodies

Highest Level Practitioner

One-pointed Yoga	Continuous, effortless concentration
Yoga Free from Projection	Completely free of all delusions about phenomena
Yoga of One Taste	Subtle apprehension of non-duality
Yoga Free of Meditation and Non-meditation	Perfect, complete enlightenment

The highest level of practitioner is able to hold that one-pointed focus at all times—not just during a meditative session, but between sessions as well. Even in sleep, focus remains on that object effortlessly. At that point, there may arise in the mind of such a practitioner the mistaken thought that the fourth, the highest, level of practice has been attained.

However, this is not true. What has actually been attained is the ability to hold the object one-pointedly without effort, and this is not the same as the state of non-meditation.

There are other factors which define this highest level of the initial stage. This practitioner has completely turned away from worldly involvement; his sense of renunciation of the world is complete. The practitioner has lost all interest in worldly pleasures. Even the desirable aspects of the world no longer hold any attraction. Therefore, he naturally stays in an isolated place conducive to meditation without any effort or sense of being deprived. He enjoys and feels very natural in that state of meditative isolation. In addition, there is a sense of complete devotion to the spiritual teacher in this state. The mind is never directed elsewhere, but rather remains completely directed toward the spiritual teacher, toward acquiring the teachings, and toward practicing them. Beyond that, there is no interest or desire.

(2) The second level of yogic attainment is the stage of being free from projections. This is the stage where the nature of mind has been directly cognized. That is to say, ultimate reality has been seen face to face, directly experienced in a non-conceptual manner and, because of this, it is said to be free of projections. Projections are all of the conceptual elaborations used to explain or relate to the world. Having seen reality in its essence, there is no need for them. This stage also has levels that correspond to the three levels of practitioners:

Upon first directly cognizing the nature of mind, the lowest level of practitioner still has a limited view of reality. Although reality has been cognized and seen directly, the fullness of it has not been experienced. There are still many aspects of phenomena which have not been understood, and many aspects of the path which are still unclear. So there is some hesitation and doubt in the mental processes of such a person. The basic nature of reality of mind has been experienced, but this has not yet been extended so as to clear away all doubts and illusions. What is necessary at this point is full and diligent engagement in yogic practices under the direction of a qualified spiritual teacher. This will allow that initial experience of reality to expand and clear away all doubts and all illusions.

The second level of practitioner at this second stage of yogic attainment has not only seen reality face to face, but has penetrated to its very root and, in doing so, has cut off the root of delusion. At this point, with this direct realization of the nature of mind in all of its profundity, the individual becomes totally free of all fears and gains complete control over his or her mind. Having gained total control over mind, over reality itself, it is irrelevant to this practitioner whether he goes to the deepest pit of hell or ascends to the highest heaven. All reality has one taste, so there is this experience of complete freedom and unobstructedness.

The danger here is that the practitioner again thinks that he has arrived at the final goal when, in fact, there is much still left to do along the path. This state is compared to the time in the morning when the sun is just rising above the horizon and illuminates the whole world, dispelling all the darkness and shadows. There is a sense that all of the darkness has gone away. However, the rays of the sun have not yet warmed things like the rocks and the trees. Various things are still cold from the night air, yet to be warmed by the rays of the sun. Likewise, for the middle-level practitioners at this second stage of yogic realization, the understanding of reality has not penetrated the entire extent of their mental processes. They still have doubt and uncertainty about various things; there are still remnants of hesitation about the nature of reality, especially about the implications of the realization which has been experienced.

At first it seems to be a complete realization, but there gradually dawn various sorts of doubts. Questions arise. What has created this problem here or that problem there? At this stage of initial mastery, one should rely on the scriptures, the sacred writings of the words of the Buddha and the great masters, under the direction of a fully qualified spiritual teacher. In order to extend the direct realization of reality and understand all of its implications, a further accumulation of merit is required through such things as offering mandalas, further study of the sacred texts, and especially cultivation of compassion for the suffering of living beings. In a sense, this remains a mystery to a person at this stage: when the nature of mind is beginningless and endless, non-abiding and completely pure, free and unobstructed, how can living beings experience misery in this way? How can that be relieved? So, this is a process of renewing one's cultivation of loving-kindness and concern for the welfare of all living beings.

The highest practitioner who reaches this second stage of yogic realization becomes completely free of all delusions about inner and outer phenomena. In other words, this is a complete realization of the ultimate nature of all phenomena which is beyond the dichotomy of subject and object and all the elaborations of projections which are based upon that dualistic thinking. This is a powerful realization of non-duality which frees the practitioner from the illusions of the phenomenal world and from the sense of separateness from all phenomena. However, the danger here is that this can appear to be the attainment of the dharmakaya. If the practitioner holds to it as such, this is an error. So, what is needed is reliance on the words of a spiritual teacher, thereby understanding the profound and subtle nature of the ultimate level of realization and the fact that there is more work to be done to completely fill out this realization and internalize it.

There is a tendency within this category of yogic attainment, especially in those who first reach it, to feel that they have made a mistake or lost their way on the path. This is because during the initial stage of yogic attainment there is the perfect, effortless, one-pointed concentration on the object of meditation. Upon arrival at the second stage of yogic realization, there is an opening up. In contrast to the narrow focus on an object, there is an opening up of consciousness in the direct realization of the nature of mind. This can be interpreted as a loss of one-pointed concentration. That error must be transcended. One must understand that one-pointed concentration was a device, or an artifice, to allow mind to get beyond the distractions which prevent direct insight into mind. So, arriving at this second yogic state and reaching the level of the highest practitioner, there is complete freedom from all projected activity of mind, and mind becomes stabilized on reality.

At this point there are still other qualities to be developed, specifically those associated with loving- kindness and compassion and the bodhisattva attitude. So, this is what arises at this point—the bodhisattva attitude which seeks to attain perfect enlightenment in order to help all living beings transcend the misery of samsara. This feeling is no longer artificial, but rather it begins to arise spontaneously from this pure view of reality, this freedom from all projection. Realizing the misery of all living beings, great compassion arises spontaneously. At that point, one enters into a deeper and more profound practice which seeks to gain all the necessary attributes and powers to actually alleviate the miseries of limitless sentient beings.

At this highest level of practice of the second stage of realization, there is a sense that one has gone beyond the need for meditation or learning. If this were true, the practicioner would actually be at the *highest* stage of yogic realization, but this state of independence has not been reached yet. If the practitioner feels that the work of one-pointed concentration has been completed, that the freedom from projections is complete, that the loving concern for others has been developed, and nothing remains to be done, this is incorrect. There are still certain types of development which must take place.

Lord Gampopa taught this to his disciples, and it was written down by Nampopa, one of those disciples. He said that the type of pride which arises at this stage, thinking that the path has been completed and that there is nothing more to learn or to meditate on is an error. What has been attained is a complete freedom from the delusions associated with ordinary ignorance, but the delusions associated with cause and effect have not been eliminated.

The ordinary delusions are those that have to do with the perceptible world, what is directly perceived. Those which have to do with karma are things that *cannot* be directly perceived. So, the distinction here is that the obstacles to the state of perfection extend to ultimate things. In other words, there is full realization of ultimate reality by the highest level of practitioner at this stage of yogic practice. However, conventional reality has not been completely understood. What has been realized is the way things actually are, but not the way things appear. What is left to be done is to understand directly the way things appear and to unite that with the realization of the way things actually are. In other words, the conventional and ultimate must be joined together and not be seen as distinct.

(3) The next stage of yogic realization is called "the level of one taste."

For the lowest level of practitioner, there is one taste between subject and object. Mind and its objects, inner and outer, are realized in their unity. In the former state there was still a lack of integration of the realization of the conventional and the ultimate, the way things appear and the way things actually are. At this level, one has solved that problem, and everything has one taste. Samsara and nirvana are seen as one. As the great protector of living beings Nagarjuna said, "The complete understanding of samsara is nirvana. To completely realize the nature of samsara is to attain nirvana." Making a dichotomy between samsara and nirvana is ultimately a mistake. They are not of different natures.

At this point, the practitioner attains the state of non-duality, the complete realization of non-duality. He realizes that there is no one wandering in samsara. There is no being wandering in samsara, nor is there a being who attains enlightenment or attains Buddhahood. These are false dichotomies. All phenomena of samsara and nirvana have one taste, one reality. Through the force of this powerful realization, the practitioner can again make the mistake that he has reached the ultimate stage of no more learning where no more effort or meditation is necessary.

The middle-level practitioner has cut the root of all dualistic thinking. Realizing non-duality in its fullness, he sees all of reality, inner and outer, subject and object, as one. He has a sense of full enlightenment wherein nothing whatsoever—no subject or object—is separate from this directly perceived unity. This experience of vast oneness is so powerful that there is a danger of accepting this as full enlightenment and neglecting the miseries of living beings. Living beings, then, are not categorized as those who suffer the miseries of cyclic existence and those who enjoy the ultimate bliss of full enlightenment. They are all part of this completely integrated whole, or oneness, into which one has become fully integrated. That is the danger here—to lose the sense of compassionate concern for the sufferings of living beings or to experience them as part of this wondrous, non-dual reality.

For the middle-level practitioner at this stage of one taste, the realization of oneness (non-duality) can lead to a loss of contact with, or loss of understanding of, the miseries of others and a consequent separation from the basic work of bringing about the welfare of all living beings. This is a great fault that must be corrected at this stage. Again, the correction comes through full and devoted reliance on a qualified teacher who is able to point out methods to appreciate the reality of the misery of living beings. Up to this stage, the practitioner has been encouraged to perfect the meditation in isolation from the world. Now the practitioner is encouraged to re-enter the world by going to the town or marketplace to view directly living beings in all of their activities, difficulties, and ignorance. In this way, he will regain an appreciation of the nature of cyclic existence and the pressing need for someone to engage in the activities which bring about the welfare and liberation of these living beings.

The highest level of practitioner at this yogic stage of realization of one taste also realizes complete non-duality, but he does so in a more subtle way. All phenomena of samsara and nirvana are appreciated in their own aspects, even though the essence of the reality is one. Here also there is the possibility of falling into a state which is neglectful of the needs of living beings because complete oneness and non-duality are experienced. However, the realization is more subtle, so the antidote (i.e., the practice to be engaged in at this point) is somewhat different.

The medium-level practitioner needed to go into the world and perceive the misery of living beings, and thereby cultivate what is called "the compassion which apprehends living beings." Now, at this higher level, what is cultivated is compassion which is not directed toward any object. This is sometimes called "limitless compassion" because it does not focus on living beings as such, but rather is a compassion that radiates out in all directions and accomplishes the welfare of living beings according to their individual needs and dispositions. That universal compassion, developed under the guidance of a qualified spiritual teacher, is not limited to any number of living beings but is spontaneous and constant in its nature.

(4) Next is the highest of the four stages of yogic realization. This is the non-meditative stage where all effort in learning has been accomplished. It is called "non-meditative" because meditation is no longer separate from anything else. It is a state in which the meditation practice and non-meditation (or time between sessions of meditation) cannot be distinguished. Mind abides in this state at all times, so there is no longer any sense to labeling it meditation or not meditation.

Here, the lowest level of practitioner has achieved a stage which is said to be free of realization. What this means is that the meditation proceeds in an unbroken flow like a river which continues without a break. There is no sense of discovery or realization; no conception of realizing an object or arriving at a realization that something arises. It is just an unbroken stream of perfect, non-dual awareness. So it is said to be free of meditation, free of realization, but unbroken as a stream of pure enlightenment.

The middle level of practice at this highest stage of realization is such that the three bodies are manifested without exertion: the one body which is the perfection of one's own welfare (the dharmakaya) and the two bodies of the enlightened one which perfect the welfare of others (the nirmanakaya and sambhogakaya). These arise naturally through the unbroken stream of enlightenment which is free of the effort of meditation and of the interruption of discrete realizations.

Last is the highest level of practice at this highest stage of yogic realization. All good qualities have been attained, so compassion for living beings arises spontaneously and uninterruptedly, as do the activities which benefit living beings. Compassion is perfectly without objectification. It does not take up the cause of one being or another, but rather radiates out in all directions and manifests constantly according to the needs and requirements of all living beings. The realization at this stage is without any limit, without any obstructions in terms of the subject or object. The realization is complete and total. There is no longer any dependence upon causes or conditions. All the causes and conditions of total, perfect, peerless enlightenment have been met and, so, the ultimate goal is obtained.

So here we have discussed the twelve stages in the development of Mahamudra practice—from the beginning stages of realization to the attainment of the ultimate goal of perfection. This brief explanation was presented according to the tradition of Dharma Lord Gampopa.

14 Questions and Answers III

It sounds like this is all very high up there, very far away. Can I, personally, actually do this?

We all possess the innate nature of enlightenment, and therefore the attainment of the highest goal is not impossible for us. It is not even far away from us. However, it is necessary to engage in practice and exert effort. We can see this even in the world, for instance, for those who engage in sports—to become the very best in a sport requires a lot of effort, a lot of practice, a lot of exertion. And that's just to be good at playing some sort of ball game! To attain perfect enlightenment we should, of course, expect to have to make some effort and concentrate on the practice over a significant period of time. No one is saying it is easy to attain the highest state of enlightenment.

However, there is no certainty about how much any one of us has accomplished in the past, in former lifetimes leading up to the present. It could be that we have spent many lifetimes working on this path and now only need to go a little bit farther to attain the highest goal. In fact, there is no way that anyone connecting with these teachings has not exerted themselves in past lifetimes along this path of the

Buddha's teachings. It would not be possible to hear these words today if one had not engaged in strenuous effort over many lifetimes.

Understanding that, one can feel reassured that the highest state of enlightenment is within one's grasp. It will take effort, diligence, turning away from everyday affairs of the world, and concentrating on meditative practice in this lifetime. If one does that, if one becomes engaged in the practice and connected with a qualified spiritual teacher, by means of one's wishes, aspirations, and prayers and by one's willingness to follow the guidance of that teacher and engage in the practice, then one can attain the highest state of enlightenment in this very lifetime. If one does not attain it in this very lifetime but still practices diligently, one will attain it in the intermediate state, the bardo, after death. Failing even that, one will surely attain full enlightenment in the next lifetime or the one after that if one truly engages in this practice.

Now, practitioners also make the mistake of separating their practice from the rest of their lives. This is a great error. If we learn to integrate our practice in our lives, then we can make true progress no matter what type of activities we are engaged in. We have to bring all of our activities into the path. Lord Jigten Sumgön taught that meditation takes place not only in an isolated meditation hut, seated cross-legged in front of an altar, but must take place in the course of all four types of activity. The four types of activity are sitting, standing, lying down, and walking. In other words, one engages in meditative practice at all times. "In meditation" means that one is working with mind itself. Mind itself is always handy, it's always there. If we go somewhere, we don't leave it behind. So, mind is always available to work with in our practice.

For example, if we are walking along the street, we can concentrate our minds undistractedly on precisely the activity that we are engaged in and not allow mind to become distracted with the kalpanas, with conceptual thought constructions and ideas. Rather, focus on what you are doing and walk an entire block without letting mind drift off into some conceptual activity. Then, once you have arrived at the end of that block, you can renew the practice for the next block. Even when driving a car, you can focus undistractedly on that activity and cut off conceptual thoughts. This can be very helpful. Whatever you are doing, you can cultivate this meditative practice. So, if you approach meditation from the point of view that it is something to be cultivated at all times and in all activities, then you will truly make rapid process. The process will not be confined merely to an occasional meditation session.

Could you give us some instructions on sleep, in reference to lying on our left side or right side?

The sleeping posture of the Buddha is on the right side. This is considered an auspicious way to approach the practice while one sleeps. Then, focusing mind on some meditation or some visualization as one goes to sleep is very good. One can develop that, and then it can extend all through the night as one sleeps. One of Lord Jigten Sumgön's disciples, Sherab Jungne, was famous for that type of practice. He would go to sleep in that position meditating on Green Tara, visualizing her in his heart with rays of green light emanating from her. Also, we have many great practitioners in Tibet who never sleep at night.

Can you explain more about how the qualities of shamatha meditation, like concentration and clarity, affect the vipashyana meditation? How are these two related?

In the stage of mental quiescence, one avoids allowing the mind to sink down into a state of lethargy or sleepiness, and prevents mind from following any types of thoughts whatsoever, any conceptual thoughts. Thereby, one gains control over mind and has the ability to use it in the practice of vipashyana. At that point, one has to engage very actively in a relentless search for the nature of mind. This is not a relaxed state of peace or even of clarity, but rather of great effort, investigation, and analysis whereby one asks the various questions that were mentioned earlier about the nature of mind—its size, its shape, its location, its very existence. Each of these questions, as outlined before, has to be investigated thoroughly to the point of an actual determination, an actual answer.

So, whether one is practicing vipashyana or some type of deity yoga, these two go together. In all of these, it is necessary to have mental quiescence which is undisturbed by thought patterns. This mental quiescence must be employed after it has been cultivated, up until the point where one actually realizes the essential nature of mind. There is no further need for mental quiescence once one has gained insight into the ultimate reality of mind.

How do the stages of Mahamudra realization you described here relate to the bodhisattva bhumis that we read about in Gampopa's Jewel Ornament of Liberation *and other texts?*

These are somewhat different ways of looking at the same process. First of all, the fivefold Mahamudra does not relate directly to the ten bodhisattva bhumis. There is no need to look for that. Mahamudra is really talking about something a bit different, it's approaching it from the point of view of practice. What relates more closely to the bodhisattva bhumis is what was just discussed—the four levels of yogic attainment. These do relate more directly to the ten bodhisattva bhumis, and, in fact, one great teacher of the Drukpa Kagyu wrote a text which includes a discussion relating those two systems.

Without going into a great amount of detail, we could say that the first level of yogic attainment, that of one-pointed concentration, wherein the direct realization of the nature of mind first begins to dawn, corresponds to the first bodhisattva bhumi where ultimate reality is first glimpsed. However, you have the three levels of that first stage of yogic realization, that of the lesser, the middle, and greater practitioner. Technically, the first bodhisattva bhumi would correspond only to the level of the highest practitioner of the first level of yogic realization. Only at that level is reality actually glimpsed.

So the lesser and the middle level practitioner of the first stage of yogic realization would correspond to the path of preparation levels called "heat" and the level called "summit," respectively. These are the second to the highest and the highest levels of the path of preparation. This precedes the path of seeing.

The path of seeing is distinguished by the first glimpse of ultimate reality, the non-conceptual direct perception of emptiness, which is what is gained on the first level of yogic realization by the highest level of practitioner. So, what we have is the first of the bodhisattva bhumis corresponding to the highest level of practice of the first stage of yogic realization.

From there you can go up through the bhumis, starting with the lowest level of practice of the second stage of realization, that of freedom from projection; this would be the second bodhisattva bhumi. The middle level of practice at that state would be the third, and the highest level of practice at that stage is the fourth. Then, the three stages of yogic realization of one taste correspond to the fifth, sixth, and seventh. Then finally, the three levels of practice at the highest level of realization correspond to the last three, the eighth, ninth, and tenth bodhisattva bhumis. Once one has attained the eighth bodhisattva bhumi, this is considered to be the enlightenment of the Buddha, but it has to be filled out in the ninth and finally in the tenth stage.

15 Vajrasattva Purification Meditation

The Vajrasattva meditation begins with the visualization of a lotus over the very top of your head. It is important in this meditation that you think of yourself in your ordinary form, not in any transformed condition, but just as your ordinary self, complete with all of your defilements accumulated from beginningless time.

Thinking of yourself in this way, visualize a white lotus on the top of your head. In the middle of the white lotus, on top of the petals, is a white lunar disc. This is the beginning of the visualization—this lotus at the very crown of the head. The lotus has eight petals and does not necessarily have to be white. It can be red or another color, but it does have eight petals with a lunar disc on top in the center. The lotus is not located at that soft place on a baby's head where the plates of the skull come together. It's back a little bit, in the center of the top of the head. Visualize it being a little above there, so the precise spot is not critical.

The white lunar disc on top of the flower is somewhat convex so that the center is raised up. On that convex, white lunar disc is a radiant white syllable *HUNG*. It stands up on the disc as if it were a needle stuck in the top of a lunar cushion. The white syllable *HUNG* then dissolves in light and forms a vajra with five points on each end. This vajra is standing upright on the lunar cushion at this point.

In the very center part of the vajra, there is a syllable *HUNG*. The syllable *HUNG* does not appear as something placed in the center of the vajra, but rather it appears as if reflected, as if the center of the vajra were a mirror and it is reflecting an image of the syllable *HUNG*.

From this syllable *HUNG*, light radiates in all directions, very powerful and very concentrated. This light is of various colors, all the colors of the rainbow. Each ray of light has at its outermost end various offerings such as flowers, food, incense—all manner of auspicious, beautiful offerings. The light presents these offerings to all the Buddhas and Bodhisattvas in the ten directions. The offerings carried by the rainbow-colored rays of light reach all the Buddhas and Bodhisattvas, infinite in number.

They accept the offerings and, in turn, send their blessings. These come in the form of rays of light, which enter the world of cyclic existence and reach all living beings without exception, melting away and dissolving the residue of their negative activities and defilements. It's like sunrise on a winter morning when the grass is covered with frost. As the sun's rays strike the blades of grass, they melt away the frost. In this same way, these rays of blessings strike all living beings of the six realms and melt away their defilements.

Having reached all living beings and purified their defilements, the blessing-rays then return to the vajra which is on the crown of your head and dissolve. They all collect and dissolve into the syllable *HUNG* in the center of the vajra; this vajra then transforms into Vajrasattva.

Vajrasattva, white in color, is now seated on that lunar disc, which is on the lotus, which is over the crown of your head. As you visualize this, Vajrasattva's size is not critical; he doesn't have to be very large. This Vajrasattva is, in fact, the manifestation of all the Buddhas of the three times and ten directions in the form of a single deity. He is understood to be what results when the five Buddha families come together or arise in one form. He is also understood to be, in essence, undifferentiated from one's own root lama.

His color is the white of a snow mountain. When the bright sun shines on the snow mountain, you get a very brilliant, radiant white—that is the color of Vajrasattva. Vajrasattva has one face and two arms. In his right hand, held in the center of his chest at the heart level, is a crystal vajra with five points held vertically. He holds a bell at his left hip, either on the inside or outside. It is not critical exactly where he is holding the bell. For instance, there is a beautiful statue of Vajrasattva in Bodhgaya with the bell held on the outside of his left hip. Whether the bell is crystal or not is not specified. The left leg is slightly extended.

Vajrasattva wears beautiful ornaments formed of precious jewels from the wish-fulfilling tree of the great celestial paradise. His body ornaments are extremely beautiful jewels in all the colors of the rainbow. His lower garment is made from a special kind of divine silk which is radiant, in all different colors, extremely light and strong. There are said to be thirteen ornaments on his body, these being the ornaments of the body of perfect enjoyment, or the sambhogakaya Buddha. These thirteen include the eight types of jewel ornaments and the five types of divine silk garments.

The first of the silk ornaments is the head ornament, the one that comes around the ears. The second is the one that comes down over the shoulders. The third one is the one that goes outward from the waist. The fourth goes around the waist like a belt or a girdle. The last one is the lower garment of many colors.

The divine jewel ornaments are eight in number. The first is the crown across the top of the forehead. Second are the two earrings, right and left. Next is a type of necklace that goes high around the neck, not very long. Fourth is a longer necklace coming down from the neck going down the chest; it has a second loop that goes way down low as far as the knees. Although these seem separate, they are one jewel. The two upper arm ornaments make five. The two bracelets make six. The seventh are ankle bracelets and the eighth are foot ornaments around both toes.

Next is the offering to Vajrasattva. The first offering is *argam*, which is the water offered to drink. This is a special divine elixir which is said to possess the eight superior qualities of water. Next is *padyam*, a special pure water specifically for washing the feet. Next is the offering of *pushpe*, the heavenly flowers; and these are offered to adorn Vajrasattva's ears. Next is the offering of *dhupe*, incense or perfume. Next is the offering of *aloke*, illumination. This would be light of various kinds, like the sun, the moon, stars, special divine butter lamps, things like that. Next, the offering of the heavenly ointments, *ghande*. These are special ointments which have the scent of divine flowers and special medicinal properties. Specifically, certain of these ointments are given in cold weather to warm the body and others in hot weather to cool the body. Next offered is *newidye*, food. These are heavenly foods with hundreds of flavors, extremely delicious, and beautiful to look at. The final offering is *shapta*, music. This is music of various sorts by heavenly musicians, which is most pleasing to the ears of divine beings.

These offerings are of three types: outer, inner, and secret. The outer offerings are associated with the material universe—Mt. Meru, the continents, the sun and the moon, all things which are materially manifested in the universe. The inner offerings are the offerings of your own substance; that is, your own body, flesh, blood, bones, and so forth. These can be transformed in the process of offering into divine elixir. The secret offerings have to do with the union of emptiness and bliss. Then there is the offering of ultimate reality, literally the offering of suchness, in the form of undefiled, perfect, one-pointed concentration.

After the offering is the praise of Vajrasattva.

After the praise is the main visualization. At Vajrasattva's heart is a convex moon disc, in the center of which stands the syllable *HUNG*. This syllable *HUNG* is a brilliant white, almost a silvery white as if it were made of mercury. Around it, beginning with the syllable *OM* is the 100-syllable mantra which moves about the perimeter of the white lunar disc, circling in a clockwise direction as viewed from above. The syllables of the mantra are in Vajrasattva's heart on a white lunar disc, going around the syllable *HUNG*. Each syllable is standing upright just as the central syllable *HUNG* is. They go around in that circle, each of them giving off rays of white light.

The 100-syllable mantra goes around quickly when you say the recitation quickly and goes around slowly as you say it slowly. As it goes around, it radiates light in all directions, again making offerings to the Buddhas and Bodhisattvas, especially to Vajrasattva, in all directions. Rays of light come back from them and purify the defilements of living beings, transforming each and every living being into Vajrasattva, and then dissolve into the Vajrasattva over the crown of your head.

Then from the big toe of Vajrasattva's left foot comes a stream of white ambrosia, which flows down into the top of your head. It pushes out all of the defilements and obscurations from the top of your head all the way down and out of the body through the lower orifices. So, you visualize this radiant white nectar coming into the top of the head, filling the body, and pushing dark, smoky fluid (which is all the defilements and obscurations) out of the body until, in this way, the entire body is perfectly cleansed and filled with this divine elixir.

Vajrasattva's right foot is slightly extended and the left leg is in the half lotus position. From the big toe of the right foot, the purifying elixir flows from between the nail of the toe and the toe itself. It is as if this were a spigot on a barrel which you open and get a focused stream of water.

Now there is a certain difficulty which sometimes arises, especially for beginners, when we try to visualize the process of nectar coming down from the mantra in Vajrasattva's heart and going out from his big toe down into our head and purifying us of defilements and obscurations. When we think about it very hard then we're trying to imagine, "OK, he's seated on this lunar disc and under it there is this lotus and his foot is up on that disc . . . now how exactly is that stream of nectar going to reach my head?" So, we have a problem that may obstruct our meditation. It is said to be okay to visualize purifying nectar collecting in the lotus and then coming out the stem at the bottom of the lotus. The nectar is funneled down into our head and we are purified that way.

However, there is a fault here. Although this type of modification sometimes helps in our initial meditation and visualization, it fosters a misconception about the nature of this process. It's a sort of clinging to our own limited reality as being ultimate. The nature of ordinary beings is that we are obstructed by physical objects like walls, trees, mountains, and things like that, whereas the nature of enlightened beings is that neither they nor their enlightened activities are obstructed by any type of material or physical obstacle. They are completely unobstructed in their activities, so it's really not necessary to be concerned about the mechanical process of receiving the flow of nectar. The power of the enlightened ones is to bestow blessings to all beings. From beginningless time, the enlightened beings have showered their blessings on living beings, but it requires a certain receptivity on the part of beings. So, because of that we can just think we are receiving directly these blessings of Vajrasattva.

In conjunction with the Vajrasattva practice, it is absolutely necessary that we practice the four antidotes which neutralize and remove the non-virtues, or negative karma. Without doing this, there is ultimately no way to stop this pernicious process of committing non-virtuous activities and building up defilements. Nor is there any way of ultimately purifying all of our former karma and misdeeds and their residue within us. So, we must engage in these four powers which act as antidotes to non-virtue.

The first of these is called the power of *regret*. Bring to mind or acknowledge the non-virtuous activities that you have performed in the past, both those which you are directly aware of and those which, through inference, you know you have done in this and past lives. Generate a very sincere sense of regret by understanding the evil nature of these activities and their terrible consequences for us in the future if we do not repent and turn away from them. So, here the first power is to regret and turn away from these activities.

Second is the power of *resolve*. This is where we make a firm determination, a decision or a vow, not to engage in these activities in the future.

The third is the power of *reliance*. This is relying on the superior, or higher, power of the enlightened beings for the resolution of our predicament. This reliance includes the Buddhas and Bodhisattvas, and the Buddha, Dharma, and Sangha. We use the first two powers in relation to this third. In other words, we openly confess what we've done in recognition of our misdeeds and their harmful nature, and resolve not to repeat them again. This confession is directed to these superior powers, the Buddhas and Bodhisattvas. Here, Vajrasattva functions in that role. So, we rely on Vajrasattva and other Buddhas and Bodhisattvas while in engaging in this process.

The fourth power is that of the actual *antidote*. This would be engaging in some type of activity which will counteract, or neutralize, the non-virtues of the past. This can be one of many types of meditations or Dharma practices, including those like the Four Thoughts that Turn the Mind from Samsara. Especially effective for this is the Vajrasattva practice in which we do this entire meditation and recite the 100-syllable mantra.

So, by engaging in this fourfold process, there is no defilement, no bad karma or misdeed, that cannot be neutralized and removed. With this visualization, the purifying nectar from Vajrasattva enters your head, pushes out all of the defilements which appear as dark fluid and leave the body from the lower orifices. Visualize that this dark fluid is flushed out of the body and falls way down and keeps on going. In this way, your body is completely purified. The defilements of body, speech, and mind are sent far away.

At this point, visualize your body as being pure and without the slightest stain or defilement, like a radiant, pure, crystal vessel. Then turn to Vajrasattva and request in prayer acknowledgment of your activity of purifying yourself. Vajrasattva acknowledges this and says that you are now purified of all of your sins and defilements. It is important that you understand this, and take that acknowledgment and hold onto it. Understand that you have been purified.

16 CONCLUSION

This is my personal advice for practice. The contemplations and meditations on impermanence and death are of the most essential importance in these practices. If you are able to generate a clear awareness of impermanence and death, then the entire practice will take on meaning and be successful. If you somehow do not understand or appreciate the significance of impermanence and death, then even if you engage in the rest of the practice very diligently, it will be difficult for you to have much success. So, focus on that basic teaching of impermanence and death. Take it in, internalize it, understand it, and then your practice will be effective.

Practicing Dharma at your present state, disposition, situation, whatever it is, until the attainment of perfect peerless enlightenment—this is what Mahamudra truly is. By practicing Mahamudra, one attains the perfect state of Buddhahood. In order to do that, the practice has to be effective. For it to be effective, we have to understand that absolutely all phenomena are interrelated, interdependent, interconnected. And because of this, the enlightened beings who have traversed this path in the past and have succeeded in attaining Buddhahood are fulfilling their vow, or obligation. In other words, they attained Buddhahood because of their great wish to help living beings. Therefore, their blessings are available to us; they always have been. Their blessings are always ready to help us, and we need these blessings in order to succeed in our practice of Mahamudra. That's what we rely upon and that is what will enable our efforts to succeed. It very definitely requires both sides—the blessings of the enlightened ones and our own receptivity, which is our aspiration and openness to their blessings.

These can be compared to an iron ring and an iron hook. We hold an iron ring, if we will just use it. If we don't hold up the iron ring of our faith, devotion, and aspiration, then the iron hook, which is the compassion and blessings of the Buddhas, will have nothing to catch onto to pull us up out of samsara to the culmination of the path of Mahamudra. So, that is our responsibility—to have openness, faith, and devotion. If we do not have it at this time, we should develop it artificially. As we practice, it will become more real and sincere and this will enable the process of connecting to the blessings of the enlightened ones to take place. Now, the ring is held on our side, the hook is held on the side of the enlightened ones. So, they are always offering the hook of their blessings to us, but unless we use our own iron ring to latch on to that, there will be no connection, and we will not receive their blessings.

It is this interconnectedness of all things which we must realize and take advantage of by becoming connected to the Buddhas and Bodhisattvas who offer us their compassionate help and blessings. Understanding the availability of their blessings, we must concentrate on the practice of developing that mind of faith and devotion which is our iron ring. Guru yoga practice is especially useful in the process of extending this iron ring, this faith and devotion. By practicing guru yoga, you develop and strengthen them and enable them to latch on to the hook of compassion.

One of the famous verses of Milarepa sums up the way the Kagyu Lineage ensures success in this practice. Milarepa said, "I, a yogin, went off from the world, entered the desolate place of cliffs and rocks, and stayed there with a mind of desolation." By desolation, he meant a mind which had turned away from the world and which had realized the precious and rare nature of the human opportunity and the faults of cyclic existence. In particular, he had realized the urgent problems of impermanence and death. With all of these things weighing on his shoulders, he turned to the compassion of his lama, who embodied the blessings of all of the enlightened ones, and did not allow his faith and devotion to waver even slightly, and they have continued in an unbroken stream from then on. So, in that way, he was able to gain these blessings and succeed in the practice.

The best advice for an ongoing religious practice, a Dharma practice which will be meaningful and successful, is to cultivate these two factors:

First, appreciation and understanding of impermanence and death. Do not turn away from them but really take them in and keep them in the forefront of your awareness at all times.

Secondly, cultivate faith, respect, and aspiration focused on a lama with an unbroken lineage, who is the embodiment of the enlightened ones.

Having done that, there is no need for other sorts of thoughts about hopes, wishes, doubts, or fears. There is no need for them, no room for them. You can let go of all of these hopes and fears. Instead, keep impermanence and death in mind, and generate more and more faith in the lineage lamas. Then, if you undertake the practice after engaging in these preliminary aspects, your practice will indeed be effective, will succeed, and will be helpful in all aspects.

In order for your practice to succeed and be beneficial for you now and in the future, you have to do more than just sample the different teachings, or just hear them and then go about your other business. Rather, understand that this is a graduated path with one thing leading to another. At each stage of this path, you have to single-pointedly grasp the practice, work on it, complete it, and then go on to the next stage. In that way, you will go higher and higher. Otherwise, if you just sample this one and that one, there will be no sense of progress.

A BRIEF BIOGRAPHY OF
HIS HOLINESS CHETSANG RINPOCHE

The founder of the Drikung Kagyu lineage of Tibetan Buddhism, Jigten Sumgön (1143-1217), belonged to one of Tibet's
most prominent families, the Kyura. Of the first twenty-four
successors of Lord Drikungpa, most belonged to the Kyura
clan. However, this hereditary lineage was discontinued after the twenty-third successor reincarnated as Drikung
Kyabgon (Protector) Chetsang, an emanation of Arya
Chenrezig. His younger brother, who succeeded him, reincarnated later as Drikung Kyabgon Chungtsang, an emanation of Padmasambhava and Arya Manjushri. In modern
times, the lineage is headed by the two Drikung Kyabgon—
His Holiness Chungtsang Rinpoche, presently residing in
Lhasa, Tibet, and His Holiness Chetsang Rinpoche, who has
his headquarters at Phiyang Monastery in Ladakh, India.

His Holiness Drikung Kyabgon Chetsang, Konchok Tenzin
Kunzang Trinley Lhundrup, was born in Lhasa on the fourth
day of the sixth lunar month in the Fire-dog year (1946). An-
nually, this corresponds to the anniversary of Lord Buddha's
first turning of the Wheel of Dharma. His father, Dundul
Namgyal, is from the Tsarong family, and his mother, Yangchen

Drolkar, is from the Rakashar family. He was indisputably recognized as the seventh Drikung Chetsang incarnation through many auspicious indications.

At a young age, His Holiness left his family to take up religious life. As he recalls, "I remember being taken to His Holiness the Fourteenth Dalai Lama when I was only four-and-a-half years old for the hair cutting and naming ceremonies. Afterwards, we went to the Drikung Kagyu main monastery for the formal enthronement ceremonies. It was not long after that, in 1950, that the Chinese Communist invasion of Tibet began." Nonetheless, the young Rinpoche was given the formal education traditional to his status.

He was taught how to read and write by His Eminence Gyabra Rinpoche and gradually received the teachings, initiations, and transmissions belonging to the general body of Kagyu lineage teachings, as well as those exclusive to the Drikung Kagyu. He also began to study the major and minor sciences, such as grammar, medicine, astrology and so forth with his tutor, Venerable Ayang Thubten Rinpoche.

"I started my philosophical studies in 1958. We began to study the *Thirty-seven Practices of Bodhisattvas* and *Guide to the Bodhisattvas' Way of Life* by Shantideva and, although Chungtsang Rinpoche was five years older than I, we studied together. This is how things remained until 1959."

Rinpoche's grandfather, a high government official, understood that the political situation in Tibet was turning from bad to worse, and strongly urged Rinpoche to leave for India. However, the monastery officials were adamant that he stay in Tibet. Sadly, his grandfather's prediction that they would regret this decision came true very quickly. Just a few months later, from the roof of Drikung Dzong, the twelve-year-old Rinpoche watched with binoculars as Chinese troops approached. Days later, the monastery was overrun.

Rinpoche remembers that he was fast asleep, when suddenly in the dark he felt someone pushing him. It was Norbu Rinpoche, who had come running in, shouting, "The army's coming, everybody has to go!" Rinpoche couldn't see anything, as it was so dark. Norbu Rinpoche helped him find his lower robe, but he couldn't find his belt anywhere. There was no time to search. So, Rinpoche just held his robe together as best he could, and they hurried downstairs. When they got downstairs, they found everyone else waiting. They were all wearing laypersons' clothing. The soldiers with guns started shouting, "Go on! Go!" but no one moved. They were all too frightened. Rinpoche recalls the moment clearly. "I started walking out on my own and Chungtsang Rinpoche followed, and then everyone else followed me and we went down together. I thought to myself that now they would shoot us, and it would be painful."

But Rinpoche was fortunate. He was not shot that day, but rather was returned to fend for himself with the other young rinpoches in the monastery for the next few months. Eventually, he was allowed to move to Lhasa with his teacher Tritsab Rinpoche, who had gotten married. He gained permission to go to school there, which he did for six years. Then the Cultural Revolution came, and he was sent to work on a farm.

This was a period of intense physical labor for Rinpoche. "I would have to get up before dawn and work until very late. On top of that, I had to cook for myself and I had to carry water from a place about fifteen minutes' walk away. In the spring and autumn, I ploughed the fields. In summer, I had to work fourteen hours a day getting firewood with a donkey. In the winter, I had to drive a cart and horse to Lhasa to bring manure to the farm." Finally, in 1975, his chance to escape came, and Rinpoche made his way to Kathmandu on foot.

The first thing he did was to search for his family. He discovered that they had all gone to the United States except for one brother, who was in Dharamsala, India. The Office of His Holiness the Dalai Lama made arrangements for him to go there. Rinpoche was officially welcomed with a mandala offering. A large number of his followers gathered there to celebrate his miraculous escape, and to plead with him to stay in India. But a week later, his father arrived to take him to the United States to reunite the family after eighteen years of separation.

Rinpoche encountered the inevitable culture shock upon his arrival in the United States. He recalled later, "When we left the airport, I couldn't see any people, only cars racing by. It was a completely different world! And after I settled down at my sister's home in New Jersey, nobody demanded that I report anywhere, nobody asked for anything." For most of the next three years, he stayed with his parents in Houston, Texas. He studied English in classes, and on his own at the library. Every afternoon for six months he worked at a McDonalds restaurant in order to improve his language skills.

While in the United States, His Holiness received many, many requests from Drikung followers to return to India and resume his duties as head of the lineage. In October 1978, he did so. Even though he had kept his monastic vows, he received them again from His Holiness the Dalai Lama. In 1979, Rinpoche led an enormous celebration of the eight hundredth anniversary of the founding of the Drikung Kagyu lineage, all the more moving because it marked the return of the lineage from the brink of extinction. Shortly thereafter, he went into the traditional three-year retreat. His retreat master, Kyunga Rinpoche, was very strict. He would say, "When you are doing prostrations, you must do full prostrations!" He never gave His Holiness any special treatment, but insisted that he do everything in the proper way.

Since then, His Holiness has continued his religious training in the various traditions of Tibetan Buddhism with many masters, irrespective of their sect. For example, Rinpoche spent three winters at a Drukpa Kagyu monastery studying their special teachings on Mahamudra, among other things. He received transmission of the Karma Kagyu lineage of the Six Yogas of Naropa from His Holiness the Sixteenth Karmapa, and the Drukpa Kagyu version of the same teachings from the Very Venerable Drukpa Thugse Rinpoche. He received the *Nying Thig Yeshe*, the highest teachings of the

Nyingma tradition, and the *Dam Ngag Dzod*, the essential teachings of all eight lineages, from His Holiness Dilgo Khentse Rinpoche.

In 1987, His Holiness made his first world tour and began his teaching career. Upon his return from that tour, he started the Drikung Kagyu Institute, an education center and monastery in Dehra Dun, India. He had to borrow money to start construction and with good fortune and the help of some generous friends, the institute was completed within five years. On November 16, 1992, His Holiness the Dalai Lama officially inaugurated the Institute. Because the Drikung Kyabgon feels that education is so important, classes began even as construction was underway. The first class had only two students, but now there are more than 140. The first three years of the curriculum are devoted to basic education. The next five years consist mainly of Buddhist philosophical studies from the sutra tradition, and in the sixth year students attend to the tantric tradition.

The Drikung Kagyu lineage has restored sixty of its monasteries in Tibet, including five nunneries. There are more than fifty monasteries in Ladakh, each with a resident lama. There are also five monasteries in Nepal, and five newly constructed monasteries in different parts of India. Drikung Dharma centers and temples have been established in Germany, Estonia, Latvia, Sweden, Malaysia, Taiwan, Chile, Canada, and throughout the United States. It can truly be said that the Drikung Kagyu lineage is once again flourishing under the care and direction of its protector, His Holiness Chetsang Rinpoche.

Long Life Prayer

for

**His Holiness the Fourteenth Dalai Lama of Tibet,
His Holiness Drikung Kyabgon Chetsang Rinpoche,
His Holiness Drikung Kyabgon Chungtsang Rinpoche, and
All of the Great Lamas in the World Today
Who Bestow upon us the Blessings of
the Sublime Dharma**

We pray for the long life of these holy and sublime
  Lamas,
Who are not to be differentiated from the exalted
  Vajradhara, the Lord who encompasses all the sacred
  lineages.
From this day until all of the vast ocean of samsara has
  been completely emptied,
May they abide secure on their pure lotus seats, free
  from the flaws of worldliness;
May they abide secure on their radiant solar seats,
  illuminating all without darkness or shadow;
May they abide secure on their luminous lunar seats,
  clearing away the darkness of ignorance.
O sublime Lamas, undifferentiated from the three
  bodies of the Enlightened One,
We pray that you abide here as the manifest embodi-
  ment of the Buddha's teachings,
We pray that you abide here on the throne of the sacred
  doctrine of the Great Vehicle,
We pray that you abide here as the sublime regents of

our teacher, Buddha Shakyamuni,
We pray that you abide here to turn the wheel of the
sublime Dharma,
We pray that you abide here for the benefit and welfare
of the living beings of the six realms,
We pray that you abide here until all realms of samsara
have been emptied,
We pray that you do not retire from this world to
accept the peace of nirvana.
Kind Lamas, mighty guardians of the sacred teachings,
may your lives in this world be secure and safe,
That you may carry the all-conquering banner of the
sacred teachings to the very pinnacle of existence,
That the solar radiance of the Dharma will illuminate
every world, whether near or far off,
That each and every being, throughout the universe,
will gain true and lasting peace, happiness and
fulfillment.

SUGGESTED FURTHER READING

The Eighth Situpa and the Third Karmapa. *Mahamudra Teachings of the Supreme Siddhas.* Trans. Lama Sherab Dorje. Ithaca: Snow Lion Publications, 1995.

Guenther, Herbert. *The Royal Song of Saraha.* Seattle: University of Washington Press, 1969.

Gyaltsen, Khenpo Konchog and Katherine Rogers. *The Garland of Mahamudra Practices.* Ithaca: Snow Lion Publications, 1986.

Gyaltsen, Khenpo Konchog and Victoria Huckenpahler. *The Great Kagyu Masters.* Ithaca: Snow Lion Publications, 1990.

Holmes, Ken and Katia. *The Changeless Nature.* Esdalemuir, Scotland: Karma Drubgyud Darjay Ling, 1985. (Translation of the *Uttaratantra*)

Kongtrul, Jamgön. *Creation and Completion.* Trans. Sarah Harding. Boston: Wisdom Publications, 1996.

Namgyal, Takpo Tashi. *Mahamudra, the Quintessence of Mind and Meditation.* Trans. Lobsang Lhalungpa. Boston: Shambhala Publications, 1986.

Wangchuk Dorje, the Ninth Karmapa. *The Mahamudra Eliminating the Darkness of Ignorance.* Trans. Alexander Berzin. Dharmasala: LTWA, 1978.

For further information about the activities of the Drikung Kagyu tradition of Tibetan Buddhism, please contact either:

Tibetan Meditation Center
9301 Gambrill Park Road
Frederick, MD 21702 USA

or

Drikung Kagyu Institute
PO Kulhan Dehra Dun
(UP) 248001 INDIA